1/2

COLLECTED
POEMS

COLLECTED
POEMS

KAROL
WOJTYLA

*Translated with an
introductory essay and notes by*
Jerzy Peterkiewicz

RANDOM HOUSE · NEW YORK

First American Edition

Copyright © 1979, 1982 by Libreria Editrice Vaticana,
Vatican City
Translation, introduction and notes © 1979, 1982 by Jerzy
Pietrkiewicz

Library of Congress Cataloging in Publication Data

John Paul II, Pope, 1920 –
Collected poems.

Poems, translated from the Polish.
I. Pietrkiewicz, Jerzy.   II. Title.
G7169.04A26   1982   891.8'517   82-40138
ISBN 0-394-52810-7

Manufactured in the United States of America
2 7 6 8 9 7 5 3

CONTENTS

The Poetic Profile of Karol Wojtyla

1

This collected edition of Karol Wojtyla's poems follows the selection published in March 1979 under the title *Easter Vigil and Other Poems*. *Easter Vigil* represented the first edition of Wojtyla's poetry in book form. Two years after its appearance, the Polish edition was published in Cracow. By a strange turn of fate, then, the English renditions of the poems were for two years more available than the originals.

When Karol Wojtyla was elected Pope in October 1978, few people realized he wrote poems, since he had never published any under his own name. "Andrzej Jawień" is the name associated with his poetry from 1950, when he was already a priest, through the 1960s. The true identity of "Andrzej Jawień" was a secret well-guarded by the editors of *The Universal Weekly* and *The Sign*,* the two Catholic periodicals in which the poems kept appearing. Wojtyla's other pen name was Gruda. *Gruda* means 'a clod of earth' in Polish.

The first sequence in the present collection is 'Song of the Hidden God', written when Wojtyla was still training to be a priest and printed in an obscure Carmelite periodical in Cracow. The editor wanted to include a note to the effect that the poems were 'written by a seminarist', but Wojtyla preferred full anonymity and so there was no signature under the text.

Is the poet-priest more vulnerable than other poets because of his dual vocation? We find a significant passage in Cardinal Wojtyla's preface to an anthology of poems written by priests. He asks how 'the two vocations, the priest's and the poet's, co-exist and act on each other in the same person'. Such a question, he adds, touches on the personal secret which each poet carries in him and reveals in his writing.†

* In Polish *Tygodnik Powszechny* and *Znak,* respectively.
† *Słowa na pustyni* (Words in the Desert). London, 1971.

As a priest living in an officially atheistic society, Wojtyla had to express his growing concern about man under an oppressive regime. When "Jawień" began to publish his cycles of poems in *The Universal Weekly,* a Cracow paper subjected to stern censorship (as was anything else printed in Poland), the time was indeed harsh for the Catholic Church.

In the early 1950s the communist rulers mounted a relentless offensive against religious faith on all fronts: in schools, the press, radio, publishing and, of course, in areas directly affecting the work of the clergy, from parish priests to bishops. Stefan Wyszynski, the Primate of Poland, was arrested and kept in seclusion. Priests all over the country were sent to prison on trumped-up charges. The dark night of the spirit was then not only the mystical concept of St John of the Cross, to be contemplated by the pious: it bécame a frightening reality for every Christian in Eastern Europe.

During his two years at the *Angelicum* University in Rome, Karol Wojtyla wrote a doctoral thesis on the Spanish mystic; it was the problem of faith in St John's works that he chose to analyse*. In St John of the Cross, the thinker builds on the vision of the poet. This was, in a way, a challenge that Wojtyla had to meet in his verse. Meditation in poetry needs a stylistic treatment which allows for reiteration, thought poised on thought, with sudden leaps into paradox. Cycles of poems seem to be suited to this kind of meditative writing. From the start Wojtyla found the cyclic composition best suited to his temperament. In fact, his earliest cycle, 'Song of the Hidden God', is the longest: divided into two sequences, it contains thirty-three poems in all.

The most quotable group of poems takes its theme from the man of Cyrene, who stepped across the path of Christ's martyrdom and became involved in his drama. The cycle consists of fourteen 'profiles' of ordinary or disturbed people — for example, a car factory worker, a girl disappointed in love, a schizoid. Each of them faces himself, as it were for the first time, against the cross

---

* Entitled *Doctrina de fide apud S. Joannem a Cruce* (1948). There is a Spanish translation of this work, *La fe segun San Juan de la Cruz,* published by the Biblioteca de Autores Cristianos, Madrid, 1979. The English version, *Faith According to Saint John of the Cross,* was published in San Francisco (Ignatius Press), 1981.

which he is asked to carry. At the end we see the protagonist of all those profiles, the Cyrenean himself, and his monologue, at first confused, then filled with righteous anger, stumbles over the final question: 'Justice calls for rebellion. But rebellion against whom?' This monologue shows most clearly how a moralist under repressive rule could write a poignant comment on man's free choice. The bullies and the crowd were inseparable from the making of such a choice.

Translating the cycle, I was increasingly conscious of one particular image. The stations of the Cross are usually made in relief; therefore, as we walk along them, we are aware of profiles. When the Cyrenean takes up the cross, his profile moves closer to that of Christ's. The stations, as they follow one another, form a sequence of profiles. Wojtyla's concept is both striking and coherent precisely because of this pictorial continuity. And since there are fourteen stations of the Cross, the fourteen 'profiles' in the cycle. emphasize the analogy.

An altogether different image holds the structure of another cycle which is both shorter and far more abstract than the Cyrenean sequence. The title is indicative: 'Thought—Strange Space' (1952). Here Jacob's wrestling with the unknown is also a struggle with images: thought rebounds against thought. In this 'strange space' man is to meet the emptiness where the spirit alone is the ultimate challenge of man. The Cyrenean is in every one of us because we have to pick up our cross; Jacob, too, is part of us, wrestling with words and images, a space traveller within the mind.

> Sometimes it happens in conversation: we stand
> facing truth and lack the words,
> have no gesture, no sign;
> and yet—we feel—no word, no gesture
> or sign would convey the whole image
> that we must enter alone and face, like Jacob.

2

Wojtyla has written a number of philosophical works. It is therefore not surprising that thought and its projection should preoccupy him in poetry as a reality which words, however inadequate, have to express. 'We fight with the likeness of all things', he says, 'that inwardly constitute man.' It is, indeed, the poet's task to try to get closer to that elusive vision of the whole. For this reason I consider 'Thought—Strange Space' a very important statement in his poetic development. Another of similar significance is 'The Quarry', a poem on the meaning of work, anger and love.

Written in 1956, a year of great changes in Poland, 'The Quarry' stands out like a monument in stone, honouring man's struggle with matter. The energy locked up in rock is released by the energy condensed in human hands. And 'hands are the heart's landscape'. There is violence in the overcoming of one energy by another. 'Do stones forgive?' is a question only a poet could ask. What adds to the force of the argument is the fact that at the beginning of the German occupation of Poland Wojtyla himself worked in the quarries outside Cracow. The poem, then, is based on experience but transformed by memory and reflection many years later. The white stone shines across the years. Thought versus matter; anger and love are in the balance. In a moment of vision man appears as a Gothic building.

'The Quarry' ends with an elegy in memory of a fellow-worker who died in an accident. This is social protest in which anger has been transformed by love. Under the banner of so-called realism in Eastern Europe, industrial work of every description has been praised in countless poems. Propaganda seldom succeeds as verse. This elegy at the end of 'The Quarry' succeeds because it is a humble bow to man's sacrifice, and also a passionate commemoration of what truly mattered in young Wojtyla's experience.

Rock and its solidity. Stone and rock become familiar objects as we read his contemplative poems, and form a strange link between 'The Quarry' of 1956 and the cycle of short poems written in the autumn of 1962, during the Second Vatican Council, which Wojtyla attended as a bishop. Walking then on the marble floor of the Basilica of St Peter he again found the solidity of matter under his feet, this time charged with energy of a different kind.

We must go below the marble floor,
with its generations of footsteps,

and drill through the rock to find the man
trampled by hooves of sheep.

The floor leads to the tomb of the first pontiff of Rome. 'Marble floor' and 'The crypt', both written sixteen years before the election of October 1978, strike the reader as curiously prophetic. It is as if language itself had released the energy of a symbol from the stones with which he had struggled in the quarries. Rock at the foundation of character. Stone, *pétros* in Greek, *Petrus*, Peter—the rock under which his bones are buried.

The two poems echoed recently when the Pope, after leaving the Gemelli hospital in August 1981, went back again to the crypt, there to honour the man called Peter. The meaning of this act was obvious to everyone, but its symbolic roots lay in that poem of nine lines, 'The crypt' , written nearly twenty years earlier.

Gesture is as much a sign as a word is: semiotics recognizes the significance of ritual gestures. Wojtyla himself describes the clandestine Rhapsodic Theatre as 'the Drama of Word and Gesture'.* Both endow the best of his work with well-measured rhetorical effects.

During the work of translation one cannot help noticing words and phrases which have a special function in the author's poetic diction. The eye, the pupils of eyes in particular (*źrenice* in Polish), the light refracted, breaking in reflections, light in a deep well, all kinds of depth—these sensations of sight predominate in Wojtyla's verse. And movement is frequently expressed in the idea of passing. Streets, pavements, tired feet, men passing by. Is life mere passing or a passage—a passage different for each person, yet ending in the same reality of death? This conception is fully explored in two later cycles of poems, 'Easter Vigil, 1966', a sequence inspired by Poland's Christian millennium, and the well-sustained 'Meditation on Death' (1975), for which Wojtyla used the pen name of *Gruda*. His own position in the Church was by then elevated: he became a cardinal in 1967. In these two meditations passage has double meaning, and in its ultimate connotation becomes a Paschal mystery.

---

* The title of his article in *Tygodnik Powszechny*, 7 April 1957, published under the pen name of Andrzej Jawień.

xiii

The other characteristic of Wojtyla's vocabulary is the quest for what Hopkins called 'inscape', that is, the form-giving essence of things. Look, for instance, at the manner in which the stone of 'The Quarry' is penetrated by the rays of thought. One could go further and say that all matter transformed by energy is, in fact, the revealing of its 'inscape'. How close do we get to the spirit of the phenomenal world yielding its innermost nature under the scrutiny of a visionary or a poet?

The world is charged with hidden energies
and boldly I call them by name....
I am a giver, I touch forces that expand the mind.

These are 'a bishop's thoughts on giving the sacrament of confirmation'. Here, as in other poems, one could speak of a sacramental communion between the poet's vision and that of the priest.

3

There is a strong continuity in Wojtyla's poetic progress and this is apparent in the key words which he uses again and again, from the Eucharistic meditation, 'Song of the Hidden God' to 'Stanislas'. The repetition of words within the same text is also a frequent device. However, reiteration alone would not be effective unless the poet were to make further use of it by placing the same word in different contexts, thus bringing out its manifold meanings. This is an old technique, going back to the Bible and mystical writing. In his native literature, Wojtyla had a good model in Cyprian Norwid, a post-romantic poet who was rediscovered for Wojtyla's generation.*

Norwid, a man of genius, was, like Hopkins, aiming at the semantic revaluation of the language he inherited; hence his exper-

---

*Norwid was born in 1821. After a life of neglect and poverty, he died in 1883 in Paris, and was buried in a pauper's grave. His poetry was rediscovered and edited after his death by Miriam Przesmycki, a poet and translator, and Norwid is now regarded as the most original poet and thinker in nineteenth-century Polish literature.

iments with metre and noun compounds (for which there was no tradition in Polish poetic diction). Wojtyla, it would seem, learned much from Norwid, including the manner of gnomic verse with its double-edged questions. Ultimately, however, what mattered in this influence was the affinity of minds and a profoundly Christian belief in the redemptive meaning of life. Viewed from such a perspective, even a small object or an unimportant event may reflect that hidden truth which only too often eludes us in our hurried existence. The deeper we probe into things, the more inner likeness we discover in them. Hands, described by Wojtyla as the heart's landscape, belong to this way of seeing the physical world. Profile, too, is a sudden revelation of a person. For the poet Norwid, profile was a manifestation of God, for we can never see our creator face to face. Beauty, like lightning, illuminates the many profiles of God.

In Wojtyla's Cyrenean cycle the Son of God is met profile to profile, not face to face. At twenty-four, before his ordination, Wojtyla wrote 'Song of the Hidden God'. Despite its youthful exuberance and some slackness in style, this cycle is an impressive work, especially in the way the poet tries to establish a consistent mystical code for the paradoxes of his search after the hiding God.

You are the Calm, the great Silence,
free me then from the voice.
In the tremor of Your being let me shiver
with the wind,
borne on the ripe ears of corn.

Introducing the selection of 1979, *Easter Vigil and Other Poems*, I suggested that Wojtyla must have found as much inspiration in St John of the Cross as in the Pole Cyprian Norwid. At that time I did not know 'Song of the Hidden God' because it was published anonymously before the Jawień poems. When I came to translate it, I was gratified to see that the suggestion was not misplaced. For here we have the young Wojtyla's reliving in language an experience not unlike that of St John of the Cross in his poetic record. There are echoes of St John's paradox of negation in Wojtyla's text as, for instance, in this passage:

Slowly I take away from words

their brightness, I round up thoughts
like shadows in herds.
Slowly I infuse all with the nothingness
that waits for the day of creation.

And then:

Not filled with one day of creation
I desire a far greater nothingness....

In modern criticism we often read the poet speaking through
some adopted character. Should he choose monologue, the voice
still does not come directly from him. Such devices are familiar
enough to the readers of Browning, Pound and Eliot. From the
earliest poems onwards, Wojtyla used monologue or dialogue, the
latter often implied. This practice alone places him in the contem-
porary system of poetics.

The Cyrenean on the way to Golgotha, Jacob with his flock,
Stanislas, Bishop of Cracow, and the most lyrical persona of all,
the Samaritan woman at the well, are revealing their struggle for
self-knowledge. The actor speaks of his self: 'myself to myself too
near'; and the blind man asks, 'Will you convince us there is happiness in being blind?' Each utterance tells us something of the
human being behind the persona, whether the projected character
is the Samaritan woman or the car factory worker. What matters to
the poet is the concern; every encounter is sudden, and each man
precious.

We are all passers-by, our tired eyes register other eyes—it was
always like this—the Cyrenean, remember, happened to be passing by; Christ passed by a group of weeping women, one of them
held out a kerchief.

Now, they have all gone. You are alone.
On this linen a sign of closeness, where you hide
from your own form,
from the form of life which you cannot accept....
Yearning—hunger for closeness.
The image does not satisfy: it is a sign of distance.

Veronica's concern was what mattered in that sudden encounter,
and it mattered for all time. Similar is the concern of the first

Christian prince of Poland (in 'Easter Vigil') walking among the trees grafted for the future which he will not live to see.

From this desire to act springs the desire to engrave our thought on words. Perhaps the most interesting feature of Wojtyla's poetry is the implied dialogue, by which I mean segments of conversation embedded in the text without any formal indication that they are dialogue. This occurs in sequences of thought presented as conversations with oneself: they are broken up to imply inner dialogue by the use of parenthesis, as, for instance, in 'Meditation on Death':

in all this
there is a centrifugal flow
(man, a fragment of the world differently set in motion),
this movement does not touch the core of eternity,
it frees no one from death
(man, a fragment of the world differently set in motion).

At times this parenthetical type of argument reminds one of St Thomas Aquinas, who reasons by way of statement, objection and answer. Implied dialogue, however, may cause some difficulty for the reader if he wants to identify the speakers line by line. 'Schizoid' is such an example. There questions and answers appear to overlap. The same is true of the implied dialogue in the second conversation of 'Easter Vigil': 'the meaning of things' in history is argued between a believer and a materialist. In the original Polish, dashes indicate a change of speaker (this would not be clear in English), but occasionally one wonders about the shift in emphasis — who is scoring a point? This, I believe, is intentional. Wojtyla's own writing for the theatre favored 'a many-voiced monologue',* as if he wished to weld unspoken thoughts to the thoughts already encapsulated in words. A technique of this kind must, by virtue of repetitions or echoes, blur the outlines of direct speech. For we are passers-by in the city of language as well.

Useless words, you feel. It is thought
that places you deep in the luminosity of things,

* This phrase was first coined by Norwid for his experimental play *Zwolon* (1851).

and you have to seek for them the ever-deepening space in yourself.

In his early 'Song of the Hidden God' Wojtyla the poet expressed, quite poignantly, his own helplessness in the search of the God who speaks in silences:

I beseech you, Lord, leave me
and my fallible thoughts,
put me not to the test of weakness,
the test of incapacity....

If the heart enclosed the world,
and the world went up in flames,
even if I spent myself,
nothing could I give, I know.

The mystic's own paradox is that he is always at a loss, even when he has glimpsed a brilliant meteor falling across his field of vision. Poor St John in his Toledo prison, *balbuciendo:* the stammering catcher of God's secrets.

4

When I think —my Country—I still hear
the swishing scythe, it strikes the wall of wheat,
merging into one profile with the arched sky; the light stoops.

One of Karol Wojtyla's prose poems, 'Thinking my Country' (1974), evokes the rural world he knew so well. Here Goethe's dictum applies admirably: if we want to understand a poet, we should go to his land.

I did that in June 1979, soon after the Pope's visit to his birthplace, Wadowice. Driving through the villages where his portraits were still on view in the windows of freshly painted cottages, I had a sense of communion with his past, an experience difficult to describe, and this in turn brought back my own sense of loss. Yes, Goethe was right: one must go to the poet's native region. The gentle hills of the lower Beskids inspire trust in nature. Near Wadowice there is a famous place of pilgrimages, Kalwaria Zebrzydowska, with its panorama stretching below the impressive church. At this sanctuary the young Wojtyla prayed before the shrine of the Virgin—one could not imagine a more harmonious atmosphere. Aesthetically, a perfect background to the poet's dreams of the past and the future.

It is important for a translator to see the places where his poet meditated and wrote. I saw the praying-desk in the chapel at the Metropolitan palace in Cracow: in the morning Archbishop Wojtyla stayed in here to work. I saw a house in the Tatras where Wojtyla sometimes used to come to rest—skiing was his favorite sport in winter, and he could, of course, write in this quiet place. A nun showed me the room where he slept and worked: a table by the window, a chair—nothing had been changed in the room since he last occupied it in 1978.

It would be presumptuous, and it is certainly too early, to attach any critical label to his type of verse. However, the act of transferring texts as complex as his from one language to another must, willy-nilly, become an act of balancing the subtleties of his thoughts and moods, weighing his texts on the scales of language. Thought (*myśl*) is a frequent word in his vocabulary, so is balance (*waga*) and scales (*szale*).

Just be back every day at six in the morning.
What makes you think that man
can tip the balance on the scales of the world?

Norwid, the poet of profiles, said this of lyrical poetry in a letter to a friend:

Perfect lyric poetry should be like a plaster cast: the slashes where form passes form, leaving crevices, must be preserved and not smoothed out with the knife. Only the barbarian removes all this from the plaster with his knife and destroys the whole.*

This quotation was my guiding light when translating. Whenever a striking metaphor or an idiosyncratic turn of phrase occurred in the text, it was relatively easy to find an equivalent in English. Hopkins, Pound or Eliot provided useful hints on occasion. More difficult to suggest were the implied silences between

* Letter addressed to Bronisław Zaleski, 15 November 1867.

the lines, or the questions posed at the end of some poems to upset the reader's habits of thought. In this Wojtyla is singularly skillful and can produce a verbal somersault at an unexpected moment. Some of his compact phrases are memorable because they contain a seed for meditation, such as these, for example:

Vision is love's space....

Death is only the sun's ray
too short on the sundial of hours....

Push aside the terror of things to be done.

As regards metre, the important thing to remember is that Polish verse is essentially syllabic; English, by contrast, is stressed. But within the Polish metrical system Wojtyla's verse is not at all typical. On the contrary, he shows a marked preference for long lines, some of them very long indeed, eighteen or twenty syllables, not common in Polish prosody.

My purpose was to convey the essential characteristics without obscuring the design of thought which dominates Wojtyla's structures. In a difficult poem like 'The Quarry' I decided to break up the lines in order to bring out the function of stress (the opening lines, for example, seem to suggest the regular beat of hammers). Otherwise the very length of the verses would obscure the poetic argument which is all-important in this remarkable philosophic deliberation. By contrast, the early cycle 'Song of the Hidden God', which is simpler in texture, required a different treatment. Here a few echoes from St John of the Cross helped to shape the idiom of exaltation. Each decision had to be balanced against the central intention of a translated text. It is always the mind behind the text that one wants to bring closer to the reader.

As to the mood or moods which the original inspires, the translator has to rely on his intuition and on his knowledge of those elusive elements which make up the ethos of a nation. Coming from the same generation and background as the author was invaluable in work of this kind. Unfortunately, few non-Poles can benefit from the knowledge of the Polish literary tradition which is both old and sophisticated, with poetry its chief glory. Introducing *Easter Vigil and Other Poems* three years ago, I said: 'This is poetry of thought, sometimes difficult, yet always ready for dialogue with another mind. And the heart that inspires the thought beats with compassion for Simon the Cyrenean, Mary Magdalene and the Samaritan woman, in whose shadows we still live.'

At the end of his labors a translator can only hope for the reader's sympathetic participation. And then the profile of the poet will be visible in the words carried across the frontier of language.

Jerzy Peterkiewicz
St Michael's Day, September 1981

COLLECTED
POEMS

Over this your white grave

Over this your white grave
the flowers of life in white –
so many years without you –
how many have passed out of sight?

Over this your white grave
covered for years, there is a stir
in the air, something uplifting
and, like death, beyond comprehension.

Over this your white grave
oh, mother, can such loving cease?
for all his filial adoration
a prayer:
Give her eternal peace –

Cracow, spring 1939

SONG OF
THE HIDDEN GOD

Shores of silence

1

The distant shores of silence begin
at the door. You cannot fly there
like a bird. You must stop, look deeper,
still deeper, until nothing deflects the soul
from the deepmost deep.

No greenery can now satisfy your sight:
the captive eyes will not come home.
And you thought life would hide you from
the other Life that overhangs the depths.

You must know – there is no return
from this flow, this embrace within the mysterious
beauty of Eternity.
Only endure, endure, do not interrupt
the flight of shadows – only endure
clear and simple – more and more.

Meanwhile you always step aside for Someone
from beyond,
who closes the door of your small room.
His coming softens with each step
and with this silence strikes
the target of the depths.

2

He is your Friend. Your memory always meanders
back to that morning in winter.
For many years you believed, knew for certain
and still you are lost in wonder.

Bent over a lamp, a sheaf of light in a knot
over your head. You look up no more,
not knowing – is he out there, or
here in the depth of closed eyes?

There, he is there. Only a tremor here,
only words retrieved from nothingness.
Oh – and a particle still remains
of that amazement which will become the essence
of eternity.

3

As long as you receive the sea,
those waving circles of the sea
into your open eyes,
you feel all depth, every frontier
drowning in you.

But your foot touches a wave
and you think: it is the sea
that dwelt in me,
spreading such calm around, such cool.

Oh, to drown! to be drowned, first leaning out,
then slowly slipping –
you can't feel steps in the ebb,
trembling you rush down.
A soul, only a human soul sunk in a tiny drop,
the soul snatched into the current.

4

The element of light is not like this.
The sea soon hides you, melts
into the silent deep.
Then the light breaks, a vertical shaft of reflection
torn from each wave as it trails.
Slowly the sea ends: brightness flows in.

And then, visible from everywhere
in mirrors far and near,
you see your own shadow.
In this Light, how can you hide?
You are not transparent enough
while brightness breathes from every side.

Look into yourself: here is your Friend,
a single spark, yet Luminosity itself.
Encompassing this spark within yourself
you see no more,
no longer feel
by what Love you are embraced.

5

Love explained all for me,
all was resolved by love,
so this love I adore
wherever it may be.

I am open space for a placid tide
where no wave roars, clutching at rainbow branches.
Now a soothing wave uncovers light in the deep
and breathes light onto unsilvered leaves.

In such silence I hide,
a leaf released from the wind,
no longer anxious for the days that fall.
They must all fall, I know.

6

For long
Someone was leaning over me –
on the line of my eyebrows
his shadow had no weight.
Like a light filled with green,
like green with no shade,
an ineffable green that rests
on drops of blood.

That leaning gesture, both cool and hot,
slides into me, yet stays overhead,
it passes close by, yet turns to faith
and fullness.

That gesture, both cool and hot,
a silent reciprocity.

Locked in such an embrace,
a gentle touch against my face:
then amazement falls,
and silence, the silence without a word,
which comprehends nothing, and the balance is nil.
And in this silence I lift
God's leaning gesture
above me still.

7

The Lord taking root in the heart is a flower
that longs for the warmth of the sun,
so flood in light from the day's inconceivable depths
and lean upon my shore.

Do not burn too close to heaven,
nor burn too far.
You should remember, heart, that gaze
in which all eternity
awaits you, dazed.

My heart, bend down. And bend your coastal towers
you sun, still misty in the depths of eyes,
bend over the unreachable flower,
one rose.

8

What does it mean that I see that much
in seeing nothing?
When the last bird sinks below the horizon,
and the wave hides it in its glass,
still lower I fall, plunging with the bird
into the tide of cool glass.

The more I strain my sight, the less I see.
Water bends over the sun to bring the reflection nearer,
the farther the shadow divides
the water from the sun,
the farther it divides the sun from my life.

For in the dark there is as much light
as there is life in the open rose,
as there is God descending from the heights
to the shores of the soul.

9

Slowly I take away from words
their brightness, I round up thoughts
like shadows in herds.
Slowly I infuse all with the nothingness
that waits for the day of creation –

So I can open up space
for your outstretched hands,
so that eternity can come closer
to receive your breath.

Not filled with one day of creation
I desire a far greater nothingness
to bring my heart's inclination
close to the breath of your Love.

10

For this moment of strange death
swept by vast tides of eternity,
for the touch of the distant heat
that makes the garden hold its breath –

The moment mingles with eternity,
the drop embraces the ocean,
and the sun's stillness in slow motion
falls into this flooded depth.

Is life a wave of wonder higher than death?
Deepest silence, flooded bay, solitary human breast.
Sailing from here into heaven
behold, when you lean out,
under the boat
children's twittering
mingles with wonder.

11

I adore you, fragrant hay, because in you
no pride ripens as in ears of corn;
I adore you, fragrant hay, because you cuddled
a barefoot baby, manger-born.

I adore you, rough wood, because I find
no complaint in your fallen leaves;
I adore you, rough wood: you covered His shoulders
with blood-drenched twigs.

And you, pale light of wheat bread, I adore.
In you eternity dwells but for a while,
flowing in to our shore
along a secret path.

12

God has come as far as that,
stopped but a step from nothingness,
so near our eyes.
It seemed to simple hearts,
to open hearts it seemed
that He was lost amidst the ears of corn.

And when the starved disciples husked the grains of wheat,
He waded deeper into the field.
Learn from me, my dear ones, how to hide,
for where I am hidden I abide.

Ears of corn, lofty in your sway,
tell, do you know his hiding place?
Where should we look, tell the way
to find Him in these fertile fields.

13

God and the universe dwelt at the heart,
but the universe was losing light,
slowly becoming the song of His Reason,
the lowest planet.

I bring you good news of great wonder, Hellenic masters:
it is pointless to watch over existence
which slips out of our hands,
for there is a Beauty more real
concealed in the living blood.

A morsel of bread is more real
than the universe,
more full of existence, more full of the Word –
a song overflowing, the sea,
a mist confusing the sundial –
God in exile.

14

Son, you will be gone. Before time began
I saw in your depth
everything that was to be.
Father, love must surge with glory.

Son, look at the swelling ears of corn
on the verge of your luminosity;
one day they will take it from you
when I give your light to the earth.

Look, Father, my eyes
are near to my love,
gazing eternally
at this day bursting with green.

They will take your hands
away from my arms – Son, can you see
this annihilation – when the day comes
I will give your bright light
to the corn on the swelling earth.

Father, my hands lost from your arms
I will weld to a tree
stripped of its green,
and with the pale light of wheat
fill this great brightness
that you change into ears of corn.

When you go, my Son – eternal Love,
who will first hold you in his closest current?

Father, I leave your sun-flooded gaze.
I choose human eyes
and meet their gaze
flooded with the light of wheat.

15

Standing before You, looking with eyes
in which the routes of stars converge.
Eyes unaware of Him who is in you,
diminishing the immeasurable brightness
in Himself and the stars.

To know even less, to believe even more:
eyelids slowly closing in the trembling light,
then with the strength of sight
push back the stars' tide, the shore
over which the day hangs.

God, you are so near:
transform our closed eyes into eyes open wide,
encircle the soul's frail breeze,
rose petals trembling
in mighty wind from every side.

16

I often think of that day of vision:
it will be filled with amazement
at the Simplicity
that can hold
the world.
And the world dwells in it, untouched
until now, and beyond.

And then the simple necessity grows
to a still greater yearning
for that one day
embracing all things
with the immeasurable Simplicity
that love's breathing can bring.

17

Take me to Ephraim,* Master, let me stay with you there
where the distant shores of silence fall
on the wings of birds,
as the greenness, as the full wave falls
undisturbed by the touch of the oar,
as wide rings spread on the water
not startled by the shadow of fear.

* Ephraim: see John xi, 54.

I thank you for giving the soul a place
far removed from the din and clamour,
where your friend is a strange poverty.
You, Immeasurable, take but a little cell,
you love uninhabited places and empty.

You are the Calm, the great Silence,
free me then from the voice.
In the tremor of Your being let me shiver
with the wind,
borne on the ripe ears of corn.

Song of the inexhaustible sun

1

Your eyes fixed on the soul,
as the sun that leans on a leaf,
making sap rich for blossom.
The good is transparent,
centred in the ray, a current.
But, Master, what will become
of the leaf and the sun? Look,
evening approaches.

2

The soul is unlike the leaf.
The leaf cannot follow the sun,
fading when its green burns out.
It is the sun that moves
further from the leaf,
the circles widen as it runs.

It's not enough for the leaf
that the day dawns every day,
the sun rises every day.
Death is only the sun's ray
too short on the sundial of hours.

3

The soul is unlike the leaf:
she can hold the sun at rest
and go down with sun's
diurnal arc in the west.

There the soul stays with the sun,
low as the sun is low,
and when the sun flows further still,
a long shadow makes them one.

But the soul breaks no horizons,
anxious for distant days:
she simply knocks at the door.
And now she has reached all,
bringing the sun each day
back to its own horizon:

4

When sorrow and evening mingle,
their colours appear alike,
colours turn to a strange drink
which I lift to my lips in fear.

To leave me less lonely in my fear
You took away the evening's dread,
and to your own eternity
You gave the taste of bread.

When out of the immeasurable
You released time –
leaning on the other shore –
You heard me weep from afar
and since the beginning knew why.

You knew that for such yearning thirst,
once quenched in your eyes,
no sunlit raptures could suffice.
They would bleed like a rose.

5

Supposing this cosmos is a branch
bent by its leafy weight,
and sunshine washes over it.
Supposing each gaze is a quiet deep
held in the palm of the hand –

Though leaves tremble, though they fall,
their reflection somewhere near,
the quiet deep will always keep
its gaze on You. The Hidden.

6

When You created these poor eyes of mine,
drawing them from the deep into your open hand,
You were thinking of that eternal gaze
enraptured by the endless deep,

and You said:
I will lower myself, brother, and never
leave your eyes in solitude.
First I will hide in the cross,
then in the ripe corn as bread.

So I think:
You lower yourself so that my arms,
distanced from the cross,
should not be alone in the cosmos.
Nor my eyes, sunk in yearning.

7

If, at its greatest, love is simple
and desire most simple in yearning,
then no wonder God desired
acceptance from simple men,
their souls made of white,
but no words for their love.

Then when He gave us love
wrapped in its simple charms –
in poverty, poverty and hay,
the Mother took the baby
and rocked him in her arms,
and in a jerkin tenderly
she tucked his little feet.

Oh, miracle, wonder of wonders,
that I with my humanity
should shield God while his love shields me
with his martyrdom.

8

In a child's single look
fixed on the gentle Host
I met the heavenly Father
looking at me with love.

My eyes
like some discovered flower
trembled before this gaze
in which the world was seen,
His glory beyond power.

Our love's yearning, said the Son,
is being fulfilled. Human eyes
take in the light, and do not falter,
in the brilliance of this light unaltered.

Oh, brightness! oh, Creator's gaze,
from which more abundant than ever
new creation is being raised:
new worlds emerge in hiding.

9

Oh, to feel this moment of nothingness,
the moment before creation,
and never depart from it:
we never depart from our shadow.

And always go back to that time
when I was nursed by your Thought alone,
and was more innocent than a child,
and deeper translucence was my own.

Today, confused by existence,
I keep forgetting my nothingness.
I wander among the distant rays
cut off from the rays that are simple.

But one look into the depth
revealing eternity, a stream
passing by the door,
and in one gaze so simple
I dwell in your Thought once more.

I am at one with myself
in the brightness that hides;
I become your Thought, and am fed
by the love inside the white heat
of Bread.

10

He often looks at me from out there,
nailing my face with his gaze.
Do you know, do you know, my brother,
how he loves us? Our Father.

But the depth of his words no one knows,
no one knows how far
the farthest reason goes,
how limitless his suffering was –
solitude on the tree of the cross.

No, not the blood on the tree
that blossomed as all labours blossom
in the bread of tomorrow:
only the Father's rejection, that sorrow
of being rejected.

For that cry: Why hast thou
forsaken me, Father, Father –
and for the weeping of my Mother –
I have redeemed on Your lips
two simple words: Our Father.

11

This depth in me is so transparent,
though my eyes are veiled by drifting mist.
Do I deserve the current's depth
as I rush on, a stream too swift.

There my Lord comes each day and stays:
a streak of blood dipped in the snow,
and recognized he recognizes,
breathing abundance he repays.

If only someone were to sweep
the mist from the lucid depth,
then it would show in what misery,
then it would show in whom he hides.

And everyone would see the light
that floods the darkened depth.
Yes, all would see it in man's heart,
the simplest of the cosmic suns.

12

There is in me a transparent land
in the shimmering of the lake:
the boat, the mooring on Genezareth,
tied to the quiet waves.

And crowds, crowds of hearts,
each captured by One Heart,
by that one heart simplest
and gentlest of all.

Then, that evening with Nicodemus,
then again, on the sea shore
where I return each day,
bewitched by Your beauty.
All this – Nicodemus,
that land, the fishermen's mooring,
the transparent depth,
and that Figure so close, so near –

all this stems from a White Point,
a point of the purest white,
encompassed in the human heart
by the red flow of blood.

13

I beg You: find me a hiding place
most inaccessible,
in the calm flow of wonder,
or at the dead of night.

I beg You: shield the side
which sinks to the dark.
I beg You: discover the side
which transfixes my sight.

I know such a hiding place where
I'd waste no spark from those suns
that burn under the eyes' horizon
fixed on the deep.

Then a miracle will be,
a transformation:
You will become me,
and I – eucharistic – You.

14

I beseech you, Lord, leave me
and my fallible thoughts,
put me not to the test of weakness,
the test of incapacity.

For there is no gratitude
that can embrace infinity,
no heart that can encircle You
with the sun's ring of red.

If the heart enclosed the world,
and the world went up in flames,
even if I spent myself,
nothing could I give, I know.

Yet day by day You multiply
my feeble ineffectual lot,
surrendering your infinity
to my fallible thought.

15

Can I ever repay my gratitude to the sea
whose quiet waves come out to seek me
as I am led astray, day after day? —
and to the sun
for not spurning me, its journey done,
and for keeping evening and dawn
not far apart?

What can I give you for the nearness which
you kindle in this immensity
like fires,
like hearts poised on their equanimity?

What can I give you for that familiarity
which you start in a child's eye
and complete in the glory, untouched
by shadows of sorrow?

And for defencelessness what reward?
It gives me day in abundance.
Am I so strong that I can last?
A creature such as I, my Lord,
you should not trust.

Can I ever repay my gratitude to the sea
whose quiet waves come out to seek me
as I am led astray, day after day?
and to the sun
for not spurning me, its journey done,
and for keeping evening and dawn
not far apart?

16

Forgive my thought, Lord, for not loving enough.
My love is so mind-manacled, forgive that, Lord;
it subtracts You from thought, leaving it cool as a stream,
where you want an embrace of fire.

But accept, Lord, the wonder that leaps from my heart –
as a brook leaps up from its source –
a sign that heat may yet burn.
So, Lord, do not spurn
even that cool wonderment.
One day You will nourish it with a burning stone:
a flame in my mouth.

Oh, do not spurn this wonder of mine, Lord,
which to You is nothing; You are Entire
in Yourself,
but for me now this is all,
a stream that tears at the shore
in muted motion,
before it can declare its yearning
to the measureless oceans.

1944

SONG OF THE BRIGHTNESS OF WATER

Jesus answered and said to her: Whosoever drinketh of
this water shall thirst again; but he that shall drink of the
water that I will give him shall not thirst for ever.
JOHN iv, 13

Looking into the well at Sichar

Look now at the silver scales in the water
where the depth trembles
like the retina of an eye recording an image.

With the broad leaves' reflection
touching your face
water washes tiredness round your eyes.

Still far from the spring.

Tired eyes are the sign
that the night's dark waters
flow through words into prayer.

(Consider how arid, how arid our souls.)

The light from the well pulsates with tears:
a gust of dreams,
passers-by think, brought them down.

The well sparkles with leaves that leap
to your eyes. Reflected green
glints round your face
in the shimmering depth.

How far to the spring?

Multitudes tremble in you, transfixed
by the light of your words
as eyes by the brightness of water.

You know them in weariness. You know them in light.

When you open your eyes deep in a wave

Transparent after fresh rain, the stones glisten
as each passing step touches them slightly.
Soon it will be evening. Banging. Doors open.
How many people will enter? How many will
thaw in the light from the windows?
Evening has come. Now and again the face
of a passer-by opens the human wall – then
window lights carry it over
to some other place nearby.
The wall now contracts, now widens; still the same.
Eyes can break out of the dark, only just –
the wall is easy.

But, I tell you, your sight alone
scarcely catches people as they flow
on the wave of fluorescent lights.
They are revealed by what is most concealed
within them, that which no flame
will burn out.

When your eyes are half-closed, space
fills again with substance beyond understanding –
the darkness of men is drawn back
cradling that goodness
which feeds you from each in the crowd
as long as you are silent,
which your shouts
turn to dust.

No, no, it is not simply you, each of you,
and were it so,
your presence not only exists, it reveals.

And yet – if eyes could only be opened
not from habit, but differently;
then, then not to forget
their vision filled with delight.

Words spoken by the woman at the well, on departing

From this moment my ignorance
closes behind me like the door
through which you entered, recognizing
all I do not know.
And through me you led many people in silence,
many roads, and the turmoil of the streets.

Later recollection of the meeting

To see like this, inwardly, none of us dares.
His recognition was different. He hardly raised his eyes.
He was a great gathering of perception –
like the well blowing the brightness of water
into a face.
He had a mirror – like the well – shining deep.
For him no need to come out of himself or
raise his eyes to guess.
He saw me in himself, possessed me
in himself.
He suffused me with ease,
burst my shame in me and the thoughts
I'd suppressed for so long.
As if he – touching a rhythm in my temples –
all of a sudden
carried that great exhaustion
in me, with such care.
Words were simple. They walked beside me
like charmed sheep.
But within me they take off:
dozing birds from their nests.

He was whole in my sin and my secret.

Tell me, this must have hurt, must have weighed
(thought-waves fall heavy, a metal lid) –
You keep silent, but today I know – open for ever
by your word – that I did not suffer in You
to my full measure.
Tell me – my love today
wants to bring back that pain,
take it from You and wind it round again
like a sharp band.

34

Too late. Every pain today
returning from You,
changes to love on its way.

Such a shortcut, such goodness of perception!
And You did not even raise your eyes.
You talked to me only with those eyes
which the well re-created
in its deep brightness.

Conversations he had within her: and the people from the wall of evening

This they seem to say,
the people from the wall of evening:
    Don't think You walk alone. You have companions
    such as I, changed by your meditation
    in us, yes, your meditation in us,
    as if a word, a frail word was simply grafted,
    grafted on to the brightness –
    yes, such as I,
    raised in the dark of trampled stars.

That woman is among the people from
the wall of evening
And He is now speaking to them
through her:
    You don't walk alone, ever.
    Not for a moment, never
    is my profile separate from you
    and in you it becomes truth,
    it always becomes truth
    and the tearing so deep,
    of your living wave.

    My face is scorched by the desert,
    deep in your souls,
    and is always blown away
    by the breathing of your tired sleep.
    Why don't you take your own cross
    out of me, as I took mine from you?
    when it was burning in your arms, hanging
    in your heavy breath.

They:
    When in this sad wall of evening
    you find our faces, slippery
    from the light of many lamps,
    like fishes' flesh –
    but blood, we have blood,
    we could strike blows with blood!
He:
    I have come to outweigh
    blood with blood,
    I have come to seek
    weariness, being like you.

The Samaritan woman

It joined us together, the well;
the well led me into you.
No one between us but light
deep in the well, the pupil of the eye
set in an orbit of stones.

Within your eyes, I,
drawn by the well,
am enclosed.

The Samaritan woman meditates

I – yes I – conscious then of my awakening
as a man in a stream, aware of his image,
is suddenly raised from the mirror and brought
to himself, holding his breath in amazement,
swaying over his light.

I was raised – how, I don't know. Yet conscious
then of myself, myself before,
now divided – only by waking?
The wall opens. I often passed through this wall
not knowing that it divided
me from myself.

Yes, I am raised. Everything seems as before:
the mules with their burdens
slithering down the hill.
The world goes up, falls down
into houses carried through deep blue air
(in vain, in vain).
Lamps light up again in the midst of awaited stars.

The burden inside that you took from me – I will sense
slowly, and measure with weariness
through seasons of struggle, trying to bring out
a small part of that simple harmony
you possess without strain
beyond measure.

Straining you planted
a particle in me. But this I know:
the inner burden you took away
is not hung in the void.
Scales will never tell its weight
or differentiate.
This undifferentiated state
I weigh and I am light again.
A flame rescued from dry wood
has no weight in its luminous flight
yet lifts the heavy lid of night.

Song of the brightness of water

From this depth — I came only to draw water
in a jug — so long ago, this brightness
still clings to my eyes — the perception I found,
and so much empty space, my own,
reflected in the well.

Yet it is good. I can never take all of you
into me. Stay then as a mirror in the well.
Leaves and flowers remain, and each astonished gaze
brings them down
to my eyes transfixed more by light
than by sorrow.

1950

MOTHER

I

First moment of the glorified body

My place flows by in memory. The silence
of those distant streets does not pass away,
held up in space like glass which limpid eyes
break into sapphire and light. Nearest
are the child's words on which silence takes wing:
Mamma – mamma –
then silence falls again into the same streets,
an invisible bird.
There I have returned many a time to memories:
from which life overflows, surging from within
with unlikely meaning,
thought and emotion balanced
as if the scales were poised in pulsing blood
leaving silence undisturbed, attuned to breathing
thought and song.

Perhaps this is prayer, my Son, and these are simple days
already beyond their measure, flowing
into the pupils of my eyes, into my weightless blood.

These are simple days, my Son,
carried from those streets where silence stands
unveiling your childish voice.

How different your words now, heard from afar.
Lips once whispered them, now they reach
into my soul as thought alone, speech
simple, immediate.

Words which grow into me

Thought breaks from spoken words
and from the face, shadows falling from high walls.
People are uplifted: only yesterday
they had quiet conversations, summoning
echoes of changes far and near.

The first moment of amazement
which witnessed you, Son of my love,
shut me out.
This moment deepens still,
transforming my whole life,
and breaks, a drop of pure wax
before fading eyes.

This moment, a whole life experienced in the word
since it became my body, was nourished by my blood,
was carried in elation –
rising in my heart, as the New Man, quietly,
when thought was held in wonder and the daily toil of hands.
This high moment is fresh again
because it rediscovers you –
only the eyelashes, the drop
where once light from eyes melted in cold air,
is no more.

Overwhelming exhaustion instead
has found its light and its meaning.

Her amazement at her only child

Light piercing, gradually, everyday events;
a woman's eyes, hands
used to them since childhood.
Then brightness flared, too huge for simple days,
and hands clasped when the words lost their space.

In that little town, my son, where they knew us together,
you called me mother; but no one had eyes to see
the astounding events as they took place day by day.
Your life became the life of the poor
in your wish to be with them through the work of your hands.

I knew: the light that lingered in ordinary things,
like a spark sheltered under the skin of our days –
the light was you;
it did not come from me.

And I had more of you in that luminous silence
than I had of you as the fruit of my body, my blood.

Mature attention

There are such moments when the first flash
reveals deep in a mother's eyes the mystery of man,
like a touch of the heart behind a thin wave of sight.
I remember such flashes, they passed without trace,
leaving just enough space in me for simple thought.

My difficult son, my great, my simple son:
in me you learned the way of all men's thought,
now in the shadow of that thought you wait
for the deeper moment of the heart,
which begins differently in every man –
in me the fullness is of motherhood,
and of that fullness it never tires.

Embraced by such a moment you feel
no change, you draw into your simplicity
all that is left in me.
If a mother knows that heart's flash
in her child's eyes, then I, in your Mystery
wholly attentive, endure.

II

John beseeches her

Don't lower the wave of my heart,
it swells to your eyes, Mother;
don't alter love, but bring the wave to me
in your translucent hands.

He asked for this.

I am John the fisherman. There isn't much
in me to love.

I feel I am still on that lake shore,
gravel crunching under my feet –
and, suddenly – Him.

You will embrace His mystery in me no more,
yet quietly I spread round your thoughts like myrtle.
And calling you Mother – His wish –
I beseech you: may this word
never grow less for you.

True, it's not easy to measure the meaning
of the words He breathed into us both
so that all earlier love in those words
should be concealed.

Space which remains in you

I often return*
to the space which is Your Son, your first Son.
Then thought takes on His form
but the eyes remain empty –
and to the lips words return, the same words
which he put on
when he wanted to stay with us.

These self-same words enfold his space
better than sight,
better than memory and heart – oh, Mother,
then you are with Him again.

Bow down with me and take –
Your Son is the taste of bread,
and beyond taste, ineffable is substance.

And now – more real than in my lips' whisper,
than in thought, sight and memory –
is the space also more really in bread?
Your arms now remember His space, the little head
snuggling to your shoulder,
for the space has remained in You,
for it was taken from You.

And shining never empty. So very present in You.
When with my trembling hands I broke the bread
to give it to you, Mother,
I stood for a moment amazed as I saw
the whole truth through one single tear
in your eye.

* Spoken by John.

48

III

The song opens

I didn't know myself, that self I found in song.
I walked among people, never parting their cares
from my simple acts, my womanly thoughts
always spoken aloud.

And when the song burst out and bell-like
embraced me, I saw how the words
discover your hiding place
as light melts at the centre of thought.
When the song stops, hear my thoughts better.

Many long days will pass among people,
different people – in my blood's even pulsing
I visit You in them, giving You no other song.
When the first song returns, it will rebound,
in deepest echo against all of creation –

to find its focus again in my lips' quiet whisper,
where it lasts longest,
endures at its simplest.

Embraced by new time

My depths are seen into, I am seen through and through.
Open to sight I rise, in that vision gently submerge.
For a long time nobody knew of this;
I told no one the expression of your eyes.

How attentive your stillness: it will always be part of me.
I lift myself towards it, will one day grow so used to it
that I will stand still, transparent as water vanishing
into a dry riverbed – though my body will remain.
Your disciples will come, and hear that my heart beat has
    stopped.

My life will no longer be weighed deep in my blood,
the road will no longer slip away from my weary feet.
New time now shines in my fading eyes:
it will consume me, and dwell with my heart.
And all shall be full at the last, and left for thought's delight.

I will open out my song and know its smallest sound,
I will open out my song intent on the whole of your life,
my song possessed by the Event so simple and clear,
which begins in every man, visibly there, yet secret.

In me it was made flesh, was revealed in song with grace,
and came to many, and in them found its own space.

1950

THOUGHT-
STRANGE SPACE

...and passed over the ford of Jaboc...and, behold, a
man wrestled with him till morning....And Jacob
called the name of the place Phanuel, saying: 'I have seen
God face to face.'...

GENESIS xxxii

I

Thought's resistance to words

Sometimes it happens in conversation: we stand
facing truth and lack the words,
have no gesture, no sign;
and yet – we feel – no word, no gesture
or sign would convey the whole image
that we must enter alone and face, like Jacob.

This isn't mere wrestling with images
carried in our thoughts;
we fight with the likeness of all things
that inwardly constitute man.
But when we act can our deeds surrender
the ultimate truths we presume to ponder?

Sentences snatched from a conversation long ago, now recollected

Pass over all this in man, but passing over
is not easy when that strange world of depth
exchanges its eyes with his, a tired pulse
trembling at his fingertips. Is not all this
your proof that streets are passing too quickly
under his wornout steps?

And yet in these streets he has found his rhythm
which continually traps him, lures him away
from the profoundest tasks, half of him revealed
and half left to the contours of dusk.
Don't liken this to the horizon
always pushing him back from his own grandeur
enclosed in the narrows of days.
For this rhythm is the widest contour,
embracing all in him,
you cannot rob him of this rhythm,
it is so much his own.

Our conversation stumbles on, the hurdles of pain increase.
You say one always suffers for cardinal change.
You say, man will awake in the depths of his hardest tasks.
You are right. How immeasurably right your reason.
But man suffers most, I think, deprived of his vision.

Words' resistance to thought

If he suffers, deprived of vision,
he must tear through the thicket of signs
to the word's very centre,
its weight the ripeness of fruit.

Is this the weight Jacob felt,
pressing him down
when tired stars sank within him,
the eyes of his flock?

II

Jacob

Going away slowly, Jacob knew how strong was the water,
how weak the shins of his sheep he had led from afar.
In vain he looked for a place in the stream
where he and his flock could wade across.

He was Jacob the shepherd. Amidst the powers of the earth
he had never felt strange, being so much a part within,
and the silent tower of knowledge needed no inspiration
to grow. Aware of thought, he lacked the words.

Suddenly the full night extinguished eye after eye
of sheep and camels, of children and wives.
With his tower of knowledge Jacob remained alone
but sensed that someone
was enclosing him and would not leave.

That someone – the same one – broke open
his awareness; in the same way, yet different
from the way of children, sheep and chattels.
And He did not crush them or push them down. In one whirl
of embrace they were all in Him, trembling like petals
stirred by anxiety within.

And Jacob, too, trembled in Him. Never did reality split
so suddenly. Jacob bent under
its weight, and thus helped thought to grasp
the simplest balance in the whirl of wonder.

III

Space necessary for the drops of spring rain

Rest your eyes for a moment
on the drops of fresh rain:
the greenness of spring leaves in this bright focus,
weighing the drops down, not enough space for leaves –
and though your eyes are full of wonder
you can't, you cannot open your thought any farther.

You try in vain calming it like a child
woken from sleep: Don't move away, dear thought,
from this bright focus of things,
remain in wonder!

Useless words, you feel. It is thought
that places you deep in the luminosity of things,
and you have to seek for them the ever-deepening space
in yourself.

Error

How to extract the still centre of thought?
I can bend the street to one side,
find fault in the eyes of girls, of boys
walking by;
and when the lines of cars converge
only their windscreens perhaps
capture infinity.

And people say:
our thought is bound up with the clarity of things,
our thought remains true to the power
of ordinary things.
But if still so few of them are open to us
surely our thought is not complete.

Proper weight

These words will shake everyone.
For the thought's end means
that it has to exhaust itself in things, die out
like the eye whose bright centre recharges reality
and transforms,
although it can never free what is real
from the throbbing of human time.

But when reality's weight leans over and collapses
then it fills with thought and subsides
into man's deep pit
which I rarely tread – I wouldn't know how.

But this I know:
I can't fall apart any further.
Both the vision and the Object entire inhabit
the very same pit. I speak of it seldom,
always draw a conclusion instead
about the world's proper weight
and my own innate
depth.

IV

For the companions of the road

1

If you are looking for that place
where Jacob wrestled,
do not wander to the lands of Arabia,
nor look for the brook
on maps – you'll find the tracks much nearer.
In thought's perspective let the light of things appear
more closely bound by thought and ever more simply shaped;
then the image will not scatter but have weight.

Prepare to lift it within yourself
and be wholly transformed to the substance
where silence and solitude are good.
Being alone is possible for man
since death can tear no one away
from the solitude within.

2

And yet, if ordinary things fill our days
and all the time some inseparable gesture
hides what is within the act,
we are still certain the gesture will drop
one day, and our deeds will retain
only that which most truly exists. Fact.

THE QUARRY

Material

1

Listen: the even knocking of hammers,
so much their own,
I project onto the people
to test the strength of each blow.
Listen now: electric current
cuts through a river of rock.
And a thought grows in me day after day:
the greatness of work is inside man.

Hard and cracked
his hand is differently charged
by the hammer
and thought differently unravels in stone
as human energy splits from the strength of stone
cutting the bloodstream, an artery
in the right place.

Look, how love feeds
on this well-grounded anger
which flows into people's breath
as a river bent by the wind,
and which is never spoken, but just breaks high vocal cords.

Passers-by scuttle off into doorways,
someone whispers: 'Yet here is a great force.'

Fear not. Man's daily deeds have a wide span,
a strait riverbed can't imprison them long.
Fear not. For centuries they all stand in Him,
and you look at Him now
through the even knocking of hammers.

2

Bound are the blocks of stone, the low-voltage wire
cuts deep in their flesh, an invisible whip –
stones know this violence.
When an elusive blast rips their ripe compactness
and tears them from their eternal simplicity,
the stones know this violence.
Yet can the current unbind their full strength?
It is he who carries that strength in his hands:
the worker.

3

Hands are the heart's landscape. They split sometimes
like ravines into which an undefined force rolls.
The very same hands which man only opens
when his palms have had their fill of toil.
Now he sees: because of him alone others can walk in peace.

Hands are a landscape. When they split, the pain of their sores
surges free as a stream.
But no thought of pain –
no grandeur in pain alone.
For his own grandeur he does not know how to name.

4

No, not just hands drooping with the hammer's weight,
not the taut torso, muscles shaping their own style,
but thought informing his work,
deep, knotted in wrinkles on his brow,
and over his head, joined in a sharp arc, shoulders and veins
    vaulted.

So for a moment he is a Gothic building
cut by a vertical thought born in the eyes.
No, not a profile alone,
not a mere figure between God and the stone,
sentenced to grandeur and error.

Inspiration

1

Work starts within, outside it takes such space
that it soon seizes hands, then the limits of breath.
Look – your will strikes a deep bell in stone,
thought strikes certainty, a peak
both for heart and for hand.

For this certainty of mind, this certainty of eye,
for this vertical line
you pay with a generous hand.
The stone yields you its strength,
and man matures through work
which inspires him to difficult good.

With work then it begins: the growing in the heart and the mind,
great events, a multitude of men are drawn in.
Listen to love that ripens in hammers, in even sounds.
Children will carry them into the future, singing:
'In our fathers' hearts
work knew no bounds.'

2

This inspiration will not end with hands.
Down to stone centres it descends through man's heart
and from the heart's centre the history of stones
grows large in the layers of earth.
And in man grows the equilibrium
which love learns through anger.

Neither is ever exhausted in man,
ever ceases in the shoulders' tension,
in the heart's hidden gesture.
They partake of each other, fulfilling each other,
raised by a lever which joins movement and thought
in an unbreakable circle.

If from afar you want to enter and stay in man
you must merge these two forces into a language
simple beyond words
(your speech must not break at the lever's tension:
the fulcrum of anger and love).
Then no one will ever tear You
out from the centre of man.

Participation

The light of this rough plank,
recently carved from a trunk,
is pouring the vastness
of work indivisible into your palms.
The taut hand rests on this Act
which permeates all things in man.

Man, his eyes tired, his eyebrows sharp,
and stones have edges sharp as knives.
Electric current cuts the walls,
an invisible whip. And the sun,
July sun: white fire in the stone.

My hands – do they belong to the light
that now cuts across the railway track,
the pickaxes, the fence overhead?
They belong to the heart and the heart doesn't swear
(keep heart from lips fouled by cursing).

How splendid these men, no airs, no graces;
I know you, look into your hearts,
no pretence stands between us.
Some hands are for toil, some for the cross.
The fence over your heads, pickaxes scattered on the tracks.

Beware of hollows in stone. Electric current
fells columns, pouring them like dust through a sieve.
The young look for a road. All roads
drive straight at my heart. Do stones forgive?

Let the world rest on this balance of hands.
Keep it unchanged in every explosion
of man and stone, over that fence
but a few steps away –
sometimes a child runs carelessly past.

This balance you hold all alone
is both too far and too near.
Now we stoop, now we climb
(the child is careless, might quickly run by).

There is silence again between heart, stone, and tree.
Whoever enters Him keeps his own self.
He who does not
has no full part in the business of this world
despite all appearances.

(In memory of a fellow-worker)

1

He wasn't alone. His muscles grew into the flesh of the crowd,
energy their pulse, as long as they held a hammer,
as long as his feet felt the ground.
And a stone smashed his temples
and cut through his heart's chamber.

2

They took his body, and walked in a silent line.

3

Toil still lingered about him, a sense of wrong.
They wore grey blouses, boots ankle deep in mud.
In this they showed the end.

4

How violently his time halted: the pointers on the low-voltage
    dials
jerked, then dropped to zero again.
White stone now within him, eating into his being,
taking over enough of him to turn him into stone.

5

Who will lift up that stone, unfurl his thoughts again
under the cracked temples? So plaster cracks on the wall.
They laid him down, his back on a sheet of gravel.
His wife came, worn out with worry; his son returned from
    school.

6

Should his anger now flow into the anger of others?
It was maturing in him through its own truth and love.
Should he be used by those who come after,
deprived of substance, unique and deeply his own?

7

The stones on the move again: a wagon bruising the flowers.
Again the electric current cuts deep into the walls.
But the man has taken with him the world's inner structure,
where the greater the anger, the higher the explosion of love.

1956

PROFILES
OF A CYRENEAN

And they forced one Simon, a Cyrenean, who passed by
coming out of the country, the father of Alexander and of
Rufus, to take up his cross.
MARK XV, 21

I: Before I could discern many profiles

1

A profile among trees, different among pillars
and different again in the street, melting into its wet surface.
Different is the profile of a man standing at his own door;
different a victor's profile: a Greek demigod.

I know the Cyrenean's profile best,
from every conceivable point of view.
The profile always starts alongside the other Man;
it falls from his shoulders
to break off exactly where
that other Man is most himself,
least defenceless

(he would be defenceless if
what is in him and of him
did not form a vertical line, but gave way).

Life tells me unceasingly
about such a profile, about that other Man.
(Profile becomes cross-section.)

2

Feet search the grass. The earth.
Insects drill the greenery, swaying the stream of the sun.
Feet wear down cobbles, the cobbled street
wears down feet. No pathos. Thoughts in the crowd, unspoken.

Take a thought if you can – plant its root
in the artisans' hands, in the fingers
of women typing eight hours a day:
black letters hang from reddened eyelids.

Take a thought, make man complete,
or allow him to begin himself anew,
or let him just help You perhaps
and You lead him on.

3

Why is it not so, Magdalene, Simon of Cyrene?
Do you remember that first step which you are still
taking all the time?

4

Grass waving, a green hammock, a breezy cradle of bees.
Stone slabs stand, split by a vertical ray.
You had better walk with the wave. Walk the wave – don't hurt
    your feet.
In the wave's embrace you never know you are drowning.

5

And then He comes. He lays his yoke
on your back. You feel it, you tremble, you are awake.

II: Now I begin to discern individual profiles

Melancholic

I would not carry it. And now this pain –
how much longer is it to last? –
feebly accepted at first, now like the moth
slowly eating its way through the fabric
of imagination, or like rust
wearing out iron.

Oh, to flow out of this cryptic canal
beyond the pain's lock. There is a life
so great and simple, and its depth
does not end in me. For our reality
is more magnificent than painful.
Oh, to balance it all at last
with a gesture, mature and certain!

Not to return again and again,
but to walk on, at the daily pace of hours,
carrying that whole subtle structure
so easily disturbed
within the frontiers of the brain,
itself more affected by fatigue than pain.

And to be more with Him,
more with Him, not merely with oneself.
Push aside the terror of things to be done,
may a simple act be enough.

Schizoid *

There are moments, hollow without hope;
will I ever light up a thought,
ever strike warm sparks from my heart?

Don't push me aside, don't recoil from my anger.
This isn't anger – no, no – it's only an empty shore.

The slightest weight is too much for me,
I walk on and feel I'm not moving at all.

You never stand still, remember; your strength
recharges in silence: it will find its way.
Your strength will explode.

And then without violence, not instantly wholly yourself,
you must give heart-space to your moments, space to the
    pressure of will.

There is growth in hollow stagnation;
your fever-shot eyes must not
burn it to ashes.

* *Schizotymik*: the Polish title refers to a term in Ernst Kretschmer's typology,
  denoting a person immersed in himself and isolated.

The blind

Tapping the pavement with a white stick
we create the necessary distance.
Each step costs us dear.
In our blank pupils the world dies
unrecognizable to itself:

the world of cracking noise, not colour
(only lines, murmuring outlines).
For us how difficult to become whole,
a part is always left out
and that is the part we have to choose.

How gladly would we take up the weight
of man who seizes space without a white stick.
How will you teach us there are wrongs
besides our own?
Will you convince us there is happiness
in being blind?

Actor

So many grew round me, through me,
from my self, as it were.
I became a channel, unleashing a force
called man.
Did not the others crowding in, distort
the man that I am?
Being each of them, always imperfect,
myself to myself too near,
he who survives in me, can he ever
look at himself without fear?

Girl disappointed in love

With mercury we measure pain
as we measure the heat of bodies and air;
but this is not how to discover our limits –
you think you are the centre of things.
If you could only grasp that you are not:
the centre is He,
and He, too, finds no love –
why don't you see?

The human heart – what is it for?
Cosmic temperature. Heart. Mercury.

Children

Growing unawares through love, of a sudden
they've grown up, and hand in hand
wander in crowds (their hearts caught like birds,
profiles pale in the dusk).
The pulse of mankind beats in their hearts.

On a bank by the river, holding hands –
a tree stump in moonlight, the earth a half-whisper –
the children's hearts rise over the water.
Will they be changed when they get up and go?

Or look at it this way: a goblet of light tilted
over a plant reveals unknown inwardness.
Will you be able to keep from spoiling what has begun in you?
Will you always separate the right from the wrong?

Man's thoughts

Mention no name,
any ego will do:
whatever opens and closes with the breath of the mouth,
sometime dies in the heart's climate,
walks behind man all day long,
changes light into night, heat into frost –

all this.

People live, generations are born
bearing with them crossbeams, nails, inner conflict.
Earth though not severed, withdraws from You,
and yet grows in thought, in sudden outline.

Unable to grow up
to men, different men – their truth hangs over me,
a limb of a sad tree. And still I try,
try hard sometime.
One profile I do understand,
the one which I now sing.

No, I don't bear enough, don't spread the weight enough.
Not enough. But I think over much, how often think thus.
Pass my name over.
Don't allow me to seek my own self, let
the sand blow over all trace
of my steps
in my thoughts.

Description of man

The wefts are deeply entangled. Try to untwist them,
and you will unravel yourself.
Simply look, understand, do not stare too hard
lest the abyss engulfs you
(the abyss not of being, but of thought).

Being does not engulf, it grows into a whisper:
this is thought swollen with existence,
this is you, cosmos, God.
Otherwise everything tangles your legs,
existence shrinks to a speck,
thought in the steppes of drought.

Work, simply work, and trust. Into yourself
enter only to learn about pride, your own pride
(thus humility begins).
And take care of your will.
The flood of feeling is rare,
and its violence never comprehends God.

The car factory worker

Smart new models from under my fingers:
whirring already in distant streets.
I am not with them at the controls
on sleek motorways; the policeman's in charge.
They stole my voice; it's the cars that speak.

My soul is open: I want to know
with whom I am fighting, for whom I live.
Thoughts stronger than words. No answers.
Such questions mustn't be asked out loud.
Just be back every day at six in the morning.
What makes you think that man
can tip the balance on the scales of the world?

The armaments factory worker

I cannot influence the fate of the globe.
Do I start wars? How can I know
whether I'm for or against?
No, I don't sin.
It worries me not to have influence,
that it is not I who sin.
I only turn screws, weld together
parts of destruction,
never grasping the whole,
or the human lot.

I could do otherwise (would parts be left out?)
contributing then to sanctified toil
which no one would blot out in action
or belie in speech.
Though what I create is not good,
the world's evil is not of my making.

But is that enough?

Magdalene

The spirit has shifted, my body remains
in its old place. Pain overtakes me
to last as long as my body is growing.
Now I can give it food from the spirit
where before there was only hunger.

At times love aches: there are weeks, months, years.
Like the roots of a dry tree my tongue is dry
and the roof of my mouth. My lips are unpainted.
It takes long: Truth sounding out error.

But it is He who feels
the drought of the whole world, not I.

Man of emotion

You don't really suffer when love is flooding you:
it's a patch of enthusiasm, pleasant and shallow;
if it dries up – do you think of the void?
Between heart and heart there is always a gap.
You must enter it slowly –
till the eye absorbs colour,
the ear tunes to rhythm.

Love and move inwards, discover your will,
shed heart's evasions and the mind's harsh control.

Man of intellect

Robbing your life of charm and variety,
the taste of adventure, of space, spontaneity.

How cramped are your notions, formulas, judgements,
always condensing yet hungry for content.

Don't break down my defences: they're vital to the human lot;
each road must take the direction of thought.

Man of will

Colourless moment of will yet heavy as piston's drive,
or sharp as a whip,
a moment that, on the whole,
encroaches on nobody –
or only on me.
It doesn't ripen like fruit, out of feeling,
or emerge from thought,
it just shortens the road.
When it comes I must lift it up
and this I do, on the whole.

No place for heart and thought,
only the moment exploding
in me, the cross.

III: Simon of Cyrene

Eye to eye with this Man. The street. Many faces.
Pounding in my temples as in a forge.
Nothing adventurous for me. I don't want to offend;
let me keep myself to myself.
No beggar or convict will ever break into me;
neither will God.

I want to be fair so I bargain with you bullies
over that Man
(though I would rather be back in town).
I bargain for justice –
not my lot, rightly, yet grace for him.

But I want to be fair. This is the threshold.
No, don't go beyond, don't touch my thoughts
or my heart – you'll stir nothing there. This rough handling,
this violence – and he dares, he accepts it a beggar!

Well, a fair man so far – what next?
People will come, women and children, all the same people,
and with him – me.
Who is to say which is which
when the weight knocks us both to the ground –
me and him?
I cannot stand this – justice is not made of steel.

Smash it to pieces, open it up! (Sentences must be compact,
words must speed urgently on, no well-rounded stanzas.)
Smash it and open it up.
An eye hangs above me, rays pour from the heart;
higher than the cross-beam,
the eye is so high I can't reach it.

My petty world:
justice squeezed out, rules, regulations.
Your world is so big:
the eye, the cross-beam and he.
You could overlook the pettiness in your great world,
smash my world to nothing;
bearing the cross you could bring it all to the brink.
You are accessible, broad: all men are contained in you.

No, I don't want merely to be just.
I stand on a threshold, glimpse a new world.
A crowd passes by: women, children, soldiers;
they mill round near the frontier with God.
Silence. Silence.
Justice calls for rebellion. But rebellion against whom?

1957

THE BIRTH
OF CONFESSORS

A bishop's thoughts on giving the sacrament of confirmation in a mountain village

1

The world is charged with hidden energies
and boldly I call them by name.
No flat words; though ready to leap
they don't hurtle like mountain water on stones
or flash past like trees from sight.

Take a good look at them as you would
watch insects through a windowpane.
And still, and yet – under the words' surface
feel the ground, how firm to your feet.
(This thought is composed of currents,
not of innumerable drops).

I am a giver, I touch forces that expand the mind;
sometimes the memory of a starless night
is all that remains.

2

Inward-bent, so many they are, they stand in slanting files.
A frail flower, it seems, sprouts from the street
to take root in their hearts.

3

In their features I see a field, even and white,
upturned, their temples a slope,
their eyebrows a line below.
The touch of my open hand
senses the trust.

Thought is behind it, a thought – not seeing
but choosing. In the map of their wrinkles
is there the will to fight?
Shadow moves over their faces.
An electric field vibrates.

4

Electricity here in fact and symbol.
I look through eyelashes into the eyes:
light through a transparent grove.

The surface connects with the hidden plane,
a frontier running untouched by sight;
thoughts rise to the eyes like moths to the pane,
they silently shine in the pupils – deep,
how deep are human deeds.

5

We never see spirit – eye mirrors thought;
I meet thought halfway and then turn back.
(Sour berry of silence, or sweet burden of boughs.)
The eye competes with the face,
opening it up, wiping its shadows away.

6

The shape of the face says everything
(where else such expression of being?).
How telling the eyes of a child,
constantly crossing a strange equator
(the earth remains a small atom of thought).

Invisible pressures are trapped in the atmosphere,
yet there is light enough
to approach in this dark.

7

And who is to come?

8

Everything else enclosed in itself:
grass on the crest of the wind,
an apple tree cradled in space
abundant with fruit.
Man meets Him who walks always ahead,
courage their meeting place,
each man a fortress.

Thoughts of a man receiving the sacrament of confirmation in a mountain village

1

How am I to be born?
Will I go with the light that flows
like a mountain stream,
saying: dry, dry, dry is the river bed,
then, suddenly, stumble
like a child on a taut rope,
stumble over a thought, a threshold,
the water beating my heart and taking my peace away.

Must I ask for a spring? Is it enough to walk
with the stream, never stop, never counter a wave –

And to counter – is it to confess?
Thought perhaps must first be formed, toil born
(like opening a gate against the tide,
mooring the boat to a slender stake).

2

Must my thought occupy everything, on, on to the end?
May I never think for myself, for my own sake?
Never think of myself as a *curious phenomenon*,
always recall that I am but a *casual existence*?

3

If I have truth in me, it will break out one day.
I cannot repel it: my own self I'd repel.

4 (Thoughts about a footbridge)
I take my first steps on a footbridge.
My heart – is it a footbridge throbbing in each joist?
Is thought a footbridge?
(My thoughts only trace what my heart is tracking.
Feelings, perceptions – but which fill me more?)
This footbridge is all.
And yet I grow differently,
feel the wind differently, differently sway.
Both strong and weak speak to me
and strength is the contrast:
the world leans differently
on strength and on weakness.

Is the bridge just an image of somebody crossing?
Over the deep, groping for the shore, he throbs
at the merging of currents.

In himself man feels no weight of hours:
they hang overhead, and they vanish below.

5
And yet I stand,
a profile cut from the wave
which withdraws and leaves me behind.
My motion is different:
there a shape is enclosed in transparent brackets,
here the truth is confirmed
in my own life.

6

Wait. Have patience. I will draw You
from all riverbeds, streams, springs of light,
from the roots of trees and the plains of the sun.
When all this is in me,
when I contain the dual weight of terror and hope
and reach depths translucent as sky,
then no one will say
that I simplify.

1961

THE CHURCH

(The Basilica of St Peter, autumn 1962;
11 October – 8 December)

Wall

A straight wall, a fragment of the wall; I see
the niches, flat pilasters on either side,
with figures of saints stopped as they glide,
and in a single movement show
some vast movement sweeping through us
from the open books.

And the vaults are no weight to the wall
nor are the living men who inhabit
the single rooms of their tired hearts
far away.

Even the abyss surrounding the earth now
is no burden
while man is born an infant
suckled at his mother's breast.

Abyss
Abyssus abyssum invocat *

You always see it as space
filled with cascades of air
where glass splinters reflect and glitter
like seeds planted in distant stones.

Now observe the abyss that glitters
in the eye's reflection.
We all bear it in us.
When men are gathered together
they shift the abyss like a boat
on their shoulders.

Nothing to bypass in this commotion.
Take a ray from the eye and write
your sign.
Though you see no abyss in the mind
don't imagine that it is not there.
Light may not reach your sight, but the boat
shifts on to your shoulders:
the abyss is clothed in flesh,
become Fact
in all men.

---

* 'Deep calleth on deep', Psalm xli (xlii in King James's Version).

The Negro*

My dear brother, it's you, an immense land I feel
where rivers dry up suddenly – and the sun
burns the body as the foundry burns ore.
I feel your thoughts like mine;
if they diverge the balance is the same:
in the scales truth and error.
There is joy in weighing thoughts on the same scales,
thoughts that differently flicker in your eyes and mine
though their substance is the same.

Marble floor

Our feet meet the earth in this place;
there are so many walls, so many colonnades,
yet we are not lost. If we find
meaning and oneness,
it is the floor that guides us. It joins the spaces
of this great edifice, and joins
the spaces within us,
who walk aware of our weakness and defeat.
Peter, you are the floor, that others
may walk over you (not knowing
where they go). You guide their steps
so that spaces can be one in their eyes,
and from them thought is born.
You want to serve their feet that pass
as rock serves the hooves of sheep.
The rock is a gigantic temple floor,
the cross a pasture.

* Addressed to one of the African bishops attending the Vatican Council.

The crypt

We must go below the marble floor,
with its generations of footsteps,
and drill through the rock to find the man
trampled by hooves of sheep.
They knew not whom they trampled – a passing man?
the Man who never will pass?
The crypt speaks: I am bound to the world and besieged;
the world is an army of exhausted soldiers
who will not pull back.

Synodus

They all start up again and again:
no graveyard for tiredness; even the very old,
hardly able to move on their knees, are prepared for the stadium.
Eyes both fading and young see what is whole:
the world which must come from their bodies and souls,
from the life that they give and the death they desire.
That world will come like a thief and steal all we possess.
Poor and naked, we will be transparent as glass
that both cuts and reflects.
Lashed by conscience, this vast temple its setting,
the split world must grow whole.

Gospel

Truth doesn't drip oil into wounds to stop the burning pain,
or sit you on a donkey to be led through the streets;
truth must be hurtful, must hide.
Structures contract in the brain: raised in man
a building leans; we want to straighten
not its pediment but the ground resisting far beneath
as waves resist boats.

Truth supports man. When he can't lift himself,
indeed the building weighs double.
We all find it in us, a mysterious mould;
we range over astounded streets
where the donkey is led.
(Is there less and less truth in the streets – or more?)
We look ahead calmly: we are beyond dread.

Springs and hands

We have words to lean on, spoken long ago,
still spoken in trembling for fear we should change them in any
    way.
But is this all?

For there are invisible hands that hold us
so that it takes great effort to carry the boat,
whose story, despite the shallows, follows its course.

Is it enough to dip deep in the spring,
not to seek in invisible hands?

Two cities
(epilogue)

Each of the two cities is a whole,
which cannot be carried from heart to heart;
each has to live at our heart's expense,
in each – each of us.

Unless we are wholly at one with one of the two,
we cannot exist and remain true.
(Long hours we talk of this
above the lights of the Third City,
at its best self in the evening
when the day's tinsel is cast off.)

7:40 Bethany Pza.
Broward Blvd.
$1.50

D.E. Sams, Inc
89 N. A.
NATICK, Mass 0176
1-617-653-84

Write for the Cleansing
Program. —

Colonic Board
nic Irrigation
Iorns (w.m) 88
2 y x 44
, ilt, conservation
of Foods,

Paul A. Weber
1745 N.E. 52nd St.
Ft. Laud. 33334

Cleaning Program — bed.
material — 5 180
$125 $55 Reg 7 Day
cleaning

Tues. Night —
89 N.E.
papick Mass.

Fasting Road —
call Ed Allen — Harry Langsbey

JOURNEY TO
THE HOLY PLACES

Mount of Olives *

A fragment of earth seen through leaves,
through the thicket of time, at last through the brook
that covers the bottom of a slender chalice.
The chalice was formed from a crack in the rocks.

A fragment of earth seen still through You,
or is it through me?
The dwarfed olive trees where You
could not find shelter then, nor –
And today, why do I come?
Don't be surprised. Here for one thousand
nine hundred years each gaze passes
into that one gaze which never alters.

* The title of the original is 'Oliveti'.

The desert of Judea

It's not easy to say to this land: you are beautiful.
Slopes brown with overhanging rocks
merge with inclining clouds.
Motorcars tear through the wind and the rain,
you look for a trace of green in vain.
People have left – long ago. You cannot live here.
No road leads to such places: it runs away.

And here You came, so that You need not say to this land:
you are beautiful. The place was indifferent.
You seek out people everywhere. But to seek everywhere
You had to stop in some place.
You chose this.
The whole earth comes to this one land,
and the land becomes earth
as everything becomes that which is,
through Him Who Is.

There was no meeting with earth for Him Who Is.

What took place
we call creation,
the owning of things as one's own,
endurance in existence.

Meeting means
not only touching (no thing touches You),
not just being
(what else is there in relation to Him Who Is?) –
Meeting means not just dependence
(oh, how great is our dependence
between coming into being and nothingness,
between coming into being and annihilation).

Thus were you dependent, one land among many lands, at one with the whole of earth, at one with all that is. Thus were you dependent and are dependent still.

Land of meeting, the one and only land, through which all earth became this land, as everything became that which it is through Him Who Is.

No, I cannot say to you, you are beautiful.

Meeting may mean the beginning of parting.

Oh, land, this earth in which we do not part with Him Who Is, in which we will never part – even though you ceased to be earth, even though you crumbled in the debris of your existence.

Oh, land, earth unborn in which He Who Is became Father to us. You exhausted yourself at our birth. No sign of freshness now, no beauty remains in you.

But even when you were young, you were not graceful – though in you there were odd corners full of grace.

Identities

I come across these odd corners (they are no longer what they once were). Fig-sellers spread their small sacks, boys run about, thrusting photographs under the eyes of passers-by, and stamps wrapped in shiny cellophane. In the doorways of prosperous shops, guttural voices lure you, smuggling in now an Italian, now an English word, even Polish.

To these odd corners I find my way. A place, the place is important, the place is holy. Stones have shifted many times, and many potholes have been filled in. Since those times the sand has run interminably through over and over again. Not a grain is left. But I am not looking for that identity: the identity of a place is what fills it.

I come across these places which you have filled with yourself once and for all. I do not come to fill them with my own self, but to be filled. Oh, place, you have to be carried to many, so many places.

You were transformed so many times before you, His place, became mine.

When for the first time He filled you, you were not yet an outer place; you were but His Mother's womb. How I long to know that the stones I am treading in Nazareth are the same which her feet touched when she was Your only place on earth. Meeting You through the stone touched by the feet of Your Mother.

Oh, corner of the earth, place in the holy land – what kind of place are you in me? My steps cannot tread on you; I must kneel. Thus I confirm today you were indeed a place of meeting. Kneeling down I imprint a seal on you. You will remain here with my seal – you will remain – and I will take you and transform you within me into the place of new testimony. I walk away as a witness who testifies across the millennia.

The identity of places is not just the identity of the stones which form the corner of a house, a hearth or a well (oh! the well at Sichar* – from Jacob's days, the Samaritan woman, to this very day) – the identity of a view that sight opens up for itself.

I am contained within the same landscape: the act of seeing is also a place of meeting. I am on a pilgrimage not to the stones but to a view where the places of this earth continually flow into the same bay. And it is the bay of sight. This bay cuts deep into the land. Man is the land. I am on a pilgrimage to identity. Not on a pilgrimage to those stones embedded in the same corner of the house, the same pavement, the same hearth. This is the identity of finding one's own self in landscape. Here I come on a pilgrimage. And this place is holy.

Mount Tabor: identity in the view from its summit. Where Galilee rises in each of its fields tilled with such toil, each kibbutz picked out at night in the concentration of electric lights. A chill passes and asserts my silhouette at the setting of day.

The shores of Lake Genezareth. The identity of being in Capernaum, Bethesda, or Magdala. In the shallow water at the edge of the lake I pick up a few stones. One day I will put them in the hard-working hand of a fisherman by the Notec river.†

Identity in moving through space and in being realized by it.

Identity in breathing. The places we have in common are more in us than in the earth.

---

* See the poem on p. 50.
† In Western Poland, flowing into the Warta.

One tree

Abraham came across these places in his wanderings, a man of the great encounter (*tres vidit et unum adoravit**). He brought the inner place of meeting to these outer places where the whole earth became earth-bound, a Dwelling. Abraham, the visible beginning of a new Adam.

You have to go through a desert to these places. Abraham was still looking for meadows; in the desert of his own self he saw only one Tree (*tres vidit et unum adoravit*) – he walked towards it. Oh, tree so wide spreading, grant your shade to all men, animals and plants. A whole people must repeat and repeat again the wanderings of Abraham.

Today Arab Airlines shorten this road to two hours. Have we distanced ourselves from the hardship of wanderings, transferring the barrenness of old earth to the wide open spaces? We by-pass Mount Sinai from a distance; they had the courage to walk straight ahead towards an encounter with it.

Earth, oh, Earth, answer the demands of eternal Wisdom. Place of meeting, be a desert no more, become an oasis. Should not man blossom out there where You are close? Come and bring with you the blossom of man.

Place of the blossoming of man – can we exchange You for so many blossoming cities of the past and the future? Can we exchange the places of blossoming for the one place on which the cross was planted? A people went on pilgrimage to that place, across the desert.

Above all places of meeting this is the last and the first. Earth never parts from it. In this place earth reasserts itself. The blossoming of man is not confined to cities where man's dwellings long ago outstripped the tops of trees. Homeless people in their refuge inhabit the Earth anew through the Cross.

* See Genesis xviii. The quotation is from St Augustine, *On the Holy Trinity* (Book 2, Ch. 4): 'He saw three and worshipped one.'

The cross is here no more. One cannot even see the rock on which it stood. Houses were built at random near the place where everything made sense. Architecture here is accidental and yet so full of sense. Everything that is a part or an aspect is explicable through the whole. Place of the whole, dwelling of all encounters and of all men. Outside you they are homeless.

Place of fulfilment: there the beginning of a new Adam reached its limit. This limit is a new beginning, the beginning of us all. Here I, too, began. But what blossoming follows from it? Man is born to blossom like a flower or an animal – but they live everywhere while man is homeless.

Man blossoms through cities but brings his homeless blossom to this place where every architecture is accidental. Accidental is each city, but from what does it draw its sense – drawing it like water? The cross has become for us the well of Jacob.

The place within

My place is in You, your place is in me. Yet it is the place of all
men. And I am not diminished by them in this place. I am more
alone – more than if there were no one else – I am alone with
myself. At the same time I am multiplied by them in the Cross
which stood on this place. This multiplying with no
diminishment remains a mystery: the Cross goes against the
current. In it numbers retreat before Man.

In You – how did the Cross come to be?

Now let us walk down the narrow steps as if down a tunnel
through a wall. Those who once walked down the slope stopped
at the place where now there is a slab. They anointed your
body and then laid it in a tomb. Through your body you had
a place on earth. the outward place of the body you exchanged
for a place within, saying: 'Take, all of you, and eat of this.'

The radiation of that place within relates to all the outward
places on Earth to which I came on pilgrimage. You chose
this place centuries ago – the place in which You give yourself
and accept me.

1965

EASTER VIGIL, 1966

I: Invocation

A conversation with oneself begins

Does it mean I have struck the subject which by mutual consent
people call important, weighty, proclaim this to one another?
Does it mean, counting the years, I am in agreement
with the chronicler Thietmar of Merseburg,* that I see the past
like Master Vincent,† that I want to be
in harmony with what has passed?
(Perhaps I prefer the chronicler's vision of the paths of history
to that which I see in Vislica's dark excavations.)‡

This means I have struck the roots of my own tree,
that I go deeper into its secret growth
of which I am part, its body sharing mine.

I sense that I am in the tree, and the tree is in me.

The tree is a body physical.
The history of men, such as I, looks for its own Body.

---

* Thietmar (975–1018), Bishop of Merseburg and chronicler of the Saxon
imperial house, who recorded events in early Polish history.
† Wincenty Kadlubek (c. 1150–1223), Bishop of Cracow, who wrote a history
of Poland in Latin.
‡ Wislica, a village near Kielce in south Poland, known for its early medieval
monuments.

A conversation with God begins

The human body in history dies more often and earlier
than the tree.
Man endures beyond the doors of death in catacombs and crypts.
Man who departs endures in those who follow.
Man who follows endures in those departed.
Man endures beyond all coming and going
in himself
and in you.

The history of men, such as I, always looks for the body
you will give them.
Each man in history loses his body and goes towards you.
In the moment of departure
each is greater than history
although but a part
(a fragment of a century or two,
merged into one life).

A conversation with man begins: the meaning of things

On this point we cannot agree.
He says: man is condemned only to loss
of his body. Man's history seeks nothing
but the body of things: these remain
while man dies
and generations live on them.
Things do not die a personal death,
man is left with the immortality of things.

This I say: much of man dies in things,
more than remains. Have you tried to embrace
what does not die and find for it
profile and space?

Don't speak of unknowns.
Man is not an unknown.

Man is always full of what is human.

Never separate man from things, the body
of his history. – Never separate people from Man who became
the body of their history. Things cannot save
what is utterly human – only Man.

We stand in front of our past
which closes and opens at the same time.
Do not close the oneness of comings and goings
with wilful abstraction:
life throbbed and blood dripped from them.
Return to each place where a man died; return to the place
where he was born. The past is the time of birth, not of death.

Invocation to Man who became the body of history

I call you and I seek you, oh, Man, in whom
man's history finds its body.
I go towards you and do not say 'come'
but simply 'be'.

Be where there is no record, yet where man was,
was with his soul, his heart, desire, suffering and will,
consumed by feeling, burnt by most holy shame.
Be an eternal seismograph of the invisible but real.

Oh, Man, in whom our lowest depths meet our heights,
for whom what is within is not a dark burden but the heart.
Man in whom each man can find his deep design,
and the roots of his deeds: the mirror of life and death
eyeing the human flux.

Through the shallows of history I always reach you
walking towards each heart, walking towards each thought
(history – the overcrowding of thoughts, death of hearts).
I seek your body for all history,
I seek your depth.

II: A tale of a wounded tree

1

There was an orchard all round, trees being grafted.
Mieszko* was walking in the shade, looking round.
He did not see the gardener, or the trees,
he did not see the scions.†
And he thought: I shall not taste of this fruit when it grows.
My son will, my grandchildren will and their children.
Will the orchard yield a large crop? which fruit will people
call good?

Unafraid, the gardener makes incisions in the bark.
He trusts the tree: the wounds will strengthen its life,
it will surge anew.

I have to look at myself as the trunk of a tree:
the wounded tree expands, growing through me.

2

Why should the wounded tree expand, growing through me?
Why must I look at myself as its fruit?
The root I grow from is me – I come into blossom, my own
    blossom,
it is my own beauty, my ugliness welded
into one creature;
my own good and evil filling my consciousness,
and depending on it.
When the fruit falls from the tree of history, it falls
of its own weight, ripe in existence,
leaving its mark.
And its mark heals me.

* Mieszko, the first historical ruler of Poland, who introduced Christianity in
966. 'Easter Vigil' was inspired by Poland's thousand years as a Christian state.
† The original uses the technical term for the grafted shoot.

The tree will not draw me into its arteries:
into the narrows of life.
I accept neither its bark nor the shade that it casts.

3

And yet I have accepted the wounded tree though I counter it
　　still,
accepted its growing through me,
through my grandchildren and their children,
bearing us as fruit –
fruit of incisions through the bark.

I have understood: the tree must be wounded
so that the scion should find its own place,
understood: the tree must be wounded
to let life seep through;
understood: I must open myself –
(my life's frontiers shift so that
what is not-mine becomes mine.
And should they not shift
so that mine becomes not-mine?).

4

The Tree said:
don't be afraid when I die – don't be afraid to die with me,
don't be afraid of death – look, I revive:
death only grazed my bark.
Don't be afraid to die with me and revive. The scar will heal.
Everything in it will ripen anew –
and the fruit will not fall of its own weight.
The tree will give its fruit back to Him who grafted it –
you will eat of the fruit grown upon me, the wounded tree.
Upon me, said the Tree.
I did not feel its strangeness,
the contradictions between us vanished
(fleetingly at first?).

I was walking away; the Tree stood, embracing past and future.

5

Good, I said, outgrow me, if you have the strength,
outgrow all men, or absorb them all.
(People cannot be absorbed, they can be outgrown,
then space opens up where everyone finds room –
everyone remains himself, yet begins to live anew.)

III: Seams

1

We walk on seams. Earth once appeared even, smooth.
For generations they thought her flat disc was surrounded
by water below and the sun above.
And Copernicus came: earth lost its hinges,
it now became hinged on motion.
We walk on the seams not as before
(Copernicus stopped the sun and gave the earth a push*),
we place our feet on seams, we place our thoughts on seams.
The question is their range (you are saying: I accept
the seams I can see – I want to see them all;
if I can't see them, can't touch them, I cannot accept them).

Mieszko walked on such seams: he often felt afraid.
He offered sacrifices not only from fear,
not only to outweigh fate.
When he sought his gods in the seams of the world,
in the unknowns of fate,
when he reached his gods, and fearfully uttered their names
(the oldest words in the ancestral tongue),
then it was clear: God does not live
in the seams of the world, in human entanglements of fate,
but speaks in his own tongue, his speech of simple sincerity.

God's sincerity suffused the seams of the world;
(this is a speech not of investigation or searching,
but a speech of finding).
Someone stood up and spoke. Words were human, slavonic.
The world in them was important and unimportant.
Death was severe and full of promise.

* This line invokes a popular couplet about Copernicus the Pole.

2

Bind thought to the seams of the world –
but free the heart and open the soul!
The body will die and rise again:
life confirmed beyond life.
(When you endeavour to understand this
in the deadly struggles of the Slavs,
let me look through the seams of the soul, my own soul,
back to the souls of the Vistulans and Polans.*)

The seam of souls is word, is speech,
mutual speech. Let us name this – baptism
(when God emerged from the seams of the world,
from the entanglements of human fate)
when he spoke to Mieszko so that Mieszko could reply.

Oh, this linking of persons, invisible, intangible –
surely, it must have its sign.
Oh, this drawing into Parenthood more inward
than any visible world – this drawing in by the Word:
by silence rather than speech,
this drawing in by Love which both moves and halts motion,
this drawing in – *mysterium tremendum et fascinosum*† –
it must have a sign.

We have walked in this sign for centuries. Thought does not
    cling
to seams: it becomes a seam itself, a hinge of all motion
suffusing man.

We have walked in this sign for centuries. This sign has replaced
the seam of the world and entanglements of human fate.

---

* Vistulans and Polans, tribes dominant in the formation of the Polish state.
† 'The shattering and enchanting mystery.'

IV: Development of language

I don't know those ancient words. When I turn to the written
    record
I am still far from the living words, which
a man in history filled with his breath and sound.
(Death shifted this sound behind a wall of centuries.
Record remains, the only trace for an ardent descendant
where the path breaks off – and you know it leads further . . .)
and you know it must lead to the first inspirations of language,
those discoveries in man, to which the object responds.
Inspiration and meaning in union.
When did they start throbbing in the same stream of sound
that flows in us today?
How did they carve out their simple shapes
that the spirit embodies?
Clans, tribes, a nation outlined.
                                        Long lasted the wave of births
passing through mothers' wombs, centred on the identity
of words, and handed down with life –

How did the word *God* sound on this wave, what its first
    meaning,
before it arrived at the meaning it has
in the eternal Word?
Man arrived here –
did he know he was arriving? –
is the meaning bestowed by the mind and the heart?
(When I turn to this moment, I am *I*, not *he* –
ripened the meaning of words – how does the heart
express itself?)

You who walk behind the heart,
you who uncover the roots of our growth,
you alone have brought union
to the multiplicity of words.

V: Echo of the firstborn cry

1

Did you bring the union of all our desires?
How can this union be embraced in the multiplicity of moments –
in each our will may split into good and evil
(will, our will: the firstborn cry on the lowest deck of history).
You are tender, you are feeling – each division
has its place in You, and its mark.

You have remained in us for ever in the sign of our divisions.
In the sign of our divisions Your unity is manifest,
the unity of Man and Word: in this union You go
into the divisions scattered far and wide among us,
like good seed scattered to be made fertile,
growing into richness and likewise growing
against the unity of man in the Word.

Years later, a thousand years on, we will bring You
the riches of all our desires, riches of our defeats
(will, our will: the firstborn cry echoes through the lowest deck
    of history).
Your sign, sign of our divisions became
the sign of our riches, in this sign You defend freedom:
freedom gives birth to our riches.
With our freedom You filled your sign.
Is freedom against You?

On and on, for generations, we all walk,
every one towards a meeting with the freedom which,
filled with love, does not counter love.
On and on. For generations, we all walk,
every one towards his own freedom.
Is freedom a vacuum . . .

2

(A great vacuum in man, a vacuum in history: grafted on this
vacuum are riches and poverty, victory and defeat. In this
vacuum vertical lines were breaking, horizons narrowing –
frontiers of freedom. Freedom confirmed itself again and again,
freedom outgrew men: men departed, not realizing that they
were abusing it. When they realized, they departed with a sense
of guilt – heads sometimes fell – freedom still remained a great
vacuum to be filled.)
  With our freedom You filled Your sign.

3

Let me look with my own eyes, through my own ego.
There is an ineffable closeness to my native land –
a motion that permeates centuries,
allowing generations to evolve not only what is contained
but the person in its own right.
I measure his life with my own,
and suddenly find reciprocity.
Someone else has become my measure.

VI: Ritual

1

Our earth has become a ritual,
a sign of finding in which Man was found.
But can the reconciliation with earth replace
the necessity, the compulsion of being
which is earth, each patch of earth,
above all, the one your heart chooses.

There you take root for life and for death,
and it crushes you into dust.

With effort you see through the necessity of earth,
and with effort you are yourself seen through.
It is a constant effort to raise so many people
from the compulsion of earth –
this effort is called history.

History is not resurrection,
but the constant acceptance of death:
seeing through the human sequence of dying.
History does not reach the ritual that earth has become,
this earth of ours.
Hence our love of this earth. Love does not flow from death,
it runs beyond.

And because of the love that runs beyond death
earth has become a ritual.
Because of the love that runs beyond death,
our earth has become
a ritual.

2

There is a ritual of many waters, spouting from the earth
in the likeness of plants,
rivers are the plants of this earth
as water is the earth of plants.
Rivers freeze in winter, lakes and ponds freeze.
Springs spout: the water's life will burst the ice.
Our earth will be nearer the sun,
near enough for life.
Water and trees will come to life, the earth
will come to life, will be a ritual –
leading you beyond the circle of dying which it contains.

Each spring the earth and water say: is the necessity
of life not deeper than that of dying?
Thus say the earth and water, murmuring to each other.
Can you translate their murmuring into your own speech?
How can you graft onto thought
the death and life of the earth?

The ritual of waters speaks with a spring voice
as it restores the earth to life, and differently
in summer when man is parched with thirst like a riverbed,
when his body begs for cool and cleanliness –
then he absorbs the ritual of waters.
Here he finds an equilibrium. Man passes
into the inner equilibrium of water –
a course of destiny in each wave merges
with the peace of water.
This peace is not stagnation.

Water speaks more of endurance than of passing.
Endure in the course of your destinies, water!
Man comprehended by water, I say to you,
you are the destiny of the earth.
Our earth has become
the ritual of the plants and of the trees;
they burst like thought ripened in wisdom.
This wisdom is the country we chose with our heart,
with the consent of the earth.

3

Man grasps the light with both hands
like someone rowing a boat:
his very substance goes through the light,
his words and his deeds.
Does he want to stay in the light?
to hold it in or give it birth?
He feels the dark, the shadow; at times he holds
a frail slice of the light in his hands
like a newborn child.
He sings it lullabies like those which nurses sing –
when silence falls, the songs shine on
till the shadow of existence enfolds the child.

Earth, you give us birth, but not enough light,
only a slice, thin and frail, sufficient
for plants and animals.
How different the light a child needs:
the nurse's embrace cannot contain his substance.
How different the light a child needs.

Faithful to you, earth, I speak of the light
you cannot give me. I speak of the light
without which no man is fulfilled,
without which you, too, earth, cannot be
fulfilled in man.

In the ritual of water and light you are present,
and silent.

Man walks with his life over the ritual,
walks over with his death.
Do you think he will stamp it down?
Man passes, people pass – they run shouting
the battlecry of life.
Out of the battle a new earth is shaped
or is it only a new death?
(while beyond man's battle earth keeps its own peace?)
Will they stamp it down?

VII: Easter vigil, 1966

This is a Night above all nights, when
keeping watch at Your grave
we are the Church.
This is the night of strife
when hope and despair do battle within us.
This strife overlays all our past struggles,
filling them all to their depths.
(Do they lose their sense then, or gain it?)
This is the Night, when the earth's ritual attains its beginning.
A thousand years is like one night:
the night keeping watch
at Your grave.

THINKING
MY COUNTRY

When I think my Country—
I express what I am, anchoring my roots.
And this is what the heart tells,
as if a hidden frontier ran from me to others,
embracing us all within a past
older than each of us;
and from this past I emerge
when I think my Country,
I take her into me as a treasure,
constantly wondering how to increase it,
how to give a wider measure to that space
it fills withal.

All round they speak with tongues

1

All round they speak with tongues, telling how successive
generations have grown, adding things old and new to the
treasure of their land.

The land became a riverbed of light kindled deep in the people;
the same rivers flowed on in the same way, and round the land
still flowed the stream of speech charged with history. The river
waters ran downhill, the stream of speech ran up aspiring to the
summit.

Every man that grew from this land was the summit, he is still
– simultaneously the summit rises above each and all, ever more
steeply it rises and ever more deeply falls into conscience.

2

All round they speak with tongues; one rings clear above the rest:
our own. It goes deep into the thought of generations, flows
round our land and becomes the roof of the house in which we
are gathered together. It is seldom heard outside that house –
(Communities of men speak around us, like islands
surrounded by the ocean of a universal human speech: there I
do not discover my own wave).

My land's assets have not spread. Even when our speech
flowed out, it flowed to vanish slowly in dried-up riverbeds.

The tongues of nations did not take up the speech of my
fathers, saying it was too difficult, superfluous.

At the great assembly of peoples we cannot speak with our
tongue. Our tongue closes us in on ourselves: shutting in, not
opening out.

3

Thus enclosed under one speech among ourselves, we exist
deeply down to our roots, waiting for the fruit of ripeness and of
crises.

Embraced day after day by the beauty of our own speech, we
do not feel bitter that they don't buy our thoughts on the
world markets because of the high price of words.

Do we not cherish the desire for a still closer exchange?

A people living in the heart of its speech remains for
generations, the mystery of thought unfathomed to the end.

I still hear

When I think – my Country – I still hear
the swishing scythe, it strikes the wall of wheat,
merging into one profile with the arched sky; the light stoops.

Then harvesters come and cast the monotony of sound
against that wall
in the violent loops of their gestures. And they cut –
they cut.

I reach the heart of the drama

1

Beyond speech an abyss opens. Is the unknown to be found in the weakness which we experienced through our fathers and have ourselves inherited?

Freedom has continually to be won, it cannot merely be possessed. It comes as a gift but can only be kept with a struggle. Gift and struggle are written into pages, hidden yet open.

You pay for freedom with all your being, therefore call this your freedom, that paying for it continually you possess yourself anew.

Through this payment we enter history and touch her epochs. Which way runs the division of generations, the division between those who did not pay enough and those who had to pay too much? On which side are we? And exceeding in so many self-determinations, did we not outgrow our strength in the past? Are we upholding the burden of history like a pillar with a crack still gaping?

2

Our country: the challenge thrown down by this land to us and to our ancestors, inspiring us to determine our common good and sing her history in our own speech, as much our own as our flag.

The song of history is fulfilled in deeds built on the rock of will. In the maturity of self-determination we judge our youth, the age of division*' and the golden age.

* The division of medieval Poland into principalities after the death of Boleslas the Wrymouth in 1139.

The loss of independence is the judgement on our golden freedom.

For centuries heroes carried this verdict in themselves: taking up the challenge of their land they entered a dark night, crying: 'Freedom is dearer than life!'

We judged our freedom with more justice than others (history raised its mysterious voice). The sacrifice of many generations burnt on the altar of self-determination: the piercing cry of freedom stronger than death.

3

Can we deny this call surging in us as a tide surges against shores too high and too steep?

Can we measure our freedom against the freedom of others – the struggle and the gift?

You who have bound your freedom with ours, forgive us.

And see how continually we rediscover freedom, ours and yours,* as a gift given and a struggle still unfulfilled.

---

* 'For our Freedom and yours', a motto carried on Polish banners during the struggles for independence.

Refrain

When I think, my Country, I look for a road running upwards,
like a high voltage current cutting through slopes. This road is in
each of us, steep and upward, not allowing us to stop.

The road follows the same slopes, returns to the same places,
becomes a great silence visiting the tired lungs of my land
evening after evening.

Thinking my Country I return to the tree

1

The tree of the knowledge of good and evil grew on the river banks of our land. Together with us it grew over the centuries; it grew into the Church through the roots of our conscience.

We carried the fruits, heavy but enriching. We felt the tree spreading, but its growing roots remained deep in one patch of earth. History lays down events over the struggles of conscience. Victories throb inside this layer, and defeats. History does not cover them: it makes them stand out.

Can history ever flow against the current of conscience?

2

In which direction did the tree branch out? Which direction does conscience follow? In which direction grows our land's history? The tree of knowledge knows no frontiers.

The only frontier is the Coming which will join into one Body the struggles of conscience and the mysteries of history: it will change the tree of knowledge into the Spring of Life, ever surging.

But every day so far has brought the same division in each thought and act, and in this division the Church of conscience grows at history's roots.

3

May we never lose that clarity before our eyes, in which events appear, lost in the immeasurable tower where man yet knows whither he is going. Love alone balances fate.

Let us not increase the shadow's measure.

A ray of light – let it fall into the hearts and shine through the darkness of generations. Let a stream of light penetrate our weakness.

We must not consent to weakness.

4

Weak is a people that accepts defeat, forgetting that it was sent to keep watch till the coming of its hour. And the hours keep returning on the great clockface of history.

This, the liturgy of history. Vigil is the word of the Lord and the word of the People, which we continually receive anew. The hours pass into the psalm of ceaseless conversion: we move towards participation in the Eucharist of the worlds.

5

To you, earth, we are descending to increase your measure in all men, earth of our defeats and of our victories; in all hearts you rise as the paschal mystery.

Earth, you will always be part of our time. Across this time, learning new hope, we move towards a new earth.

And we raise you, earth of old, as the fruit of the love of generations that outgrew hate.

Cracow, 1974

MEDITATION
ON DEATH

This cycle of poems appeared under the pen
name Gruda, which means 'a clod of earth'.

Thoughts on maturing

1

Maturity: a descent to a hidden core,
layers fall from the imagination
like leaves once locked in the trunk of their tree;
the cells grow calm – though their sensitivity still stirs;
the body in its own fulness
reaches the shores of autumn.
Maturity: the surface meets the depth;
maturity: penetrating the depth,
the soul more reconciled with the body,
but more opposed to death,.
uneasy about the resurrection.
Maturing towards difficult encounters.

2

Maturity is also fear;
the end of cultivation is already its beginning,
the beginning of wisdom is fear,
based on a different layer of the same soil
where there is no need to escape,
only space
with which we measure grandeur.

We enter this space,
we depart from that beginning,
and so we slowly return:
for maturity is within love,
transforming fear.

3

When we find ourselves at the shores of autumn,
fear and love explode their contrary desires:
fear desiring the return to what was already existence,
and still is –
love desiring the departure to the One
in whom existence finds all its future.

As we look towards the autumn shores,
the struggle in us runs along
the same divide
which every man carries in him,
when his body is the past of his own future –
every man
if he cannot link his future
with his body.

Mysterium paschale

1

You cannot stop the passing currents. They are many.
They mill around, form a field where
you yourself pass, reconciled
because after all something does surge;
the world grows round you.
Also in me
something of inheritance remains, something of promise;
the passing current is the current that surges,
and you can bear neither current to the end –
both will flow on – you will fall lower,
this you know for certain;
you turn to dust,
this you know for certain. You exist
always deathbound, bound always to the future
which always steps into your current.
But will it free you from the fields that pass?
will it seize all past from existence,
and all future too?

2

Mysterium paschale,
the mystery of Passage
in which the order of passing is reversed,
since we pass from life to death –
such is the experience, and the obviousness therein.

For passing through death towards life is mystery.
Mystery – a deep record
as yet unread to the very end,
apprehended, not contrary to being
(is death not more contrary?).

If that One unveils the record,
reads it, tests it on himself, and
Passes Over,
only then we touch the traces
and take the sacrament in which
He who went remains –
and so, still passing towards death,
we stay in that space called mystery.

3

You cannot stop the passing currents. They are many. The
world grows on, reaching towards each human death, entering
the orbit of thought, of unrepeatable atoms: (man records his
heart beats in creation's passing flux, man dies – higher than the
surging world – falls below 'the world' he carried in himself and
round himself; in his exit he is smaller, buried in the web of
creation by the dust of unrepeatable atoms,
still passing on –
no longer He,
but the World
which grows on human cinders).

4

One of us, one of many
crossed all passing currents,
changed the direction of field where everyone passes,
solitary grandeur in all creation
unrepeatable.
This Passage is called *Pascha –
mysterium*:
First they ran to a grotto with animals as in a stable –
and from afar they followed the star;
then they ran to the grave – empty,
filled with luminosity,
then they climbed from the valley, steeply from Cedron's stream
under the city's overhanging cliffs
where they had put Him to death.
And all those links in His death
(the valley, the stream, the cliffs, the city)
he has divided –
and rolls back not only the tombstone
but the whole earth,
transforming the fields of passage,
though the stream of Cedron falls as before,
and as before, the stream of blood in man's body
steers towards death.
In each he planted a place of birth,
in each he unveiled a place of life
which grows beyond the passing current,
grows, beyond death.
This place in the midst of a surging world
resists death: it also receives the resurrection
as simplest ignorance, the fulness of faith
as ferment
which gives the lie to the surging world.

Fear which is at the beginning

1

Oh, how you are bound, place of my passage,
with the place of my birth.
God's design rests on the faces of passers-by,
its depth following the course of ordinary days.

Sliding into death I unveil the awaiting, my eyes
fixed on one place, one resurrection.
Yet I close the lid of my body, and the certainty
of its decay I entrust to the earth.
You rise above it slowly, and level Your design
with the surface of each day,
and with the shadows of passers-by in afternoon streets,
in the streets of our town at dusk.
You God, you alone
can retrieve our bodies from the earth.

2

This is the last word of faith going
to meet the necessity of passing,
the word that answers the record
not contradictory to being (death is contradiction),
the word most held in suspicion, uttered
despite everyday deaths,
despite this planet's history, which became
our place of passage, the place of death,
generation after generation.

3

Allow the mystery to work in me,
teach me to act within my body
suffused with weakness like a herald prophesying death,
like a cock crowing –
Allow the mystery to work in me, teach me to act in my soul
which intercepts the body's fear
and fears for that body –
the soul still has its fear for maturity, for acts –
shadows the human spirit carries forever –
and of the depth in which it was submerged;
finally of the divine, that fear
which is not against hope.

Hope reaching beyond the limit

1

Hope rises in time
from all places subject to death –
hope is its counterweight.
The dying world unveils its life again
in hope.

Young men in short jackets, hair falling on their necks,
pass in the streets, their sharp steps
cut into the space of that great mystery which
in every one of them stretches
between his own death and his own hope;
space leaping upwards like the splash of the sun:
the stone rolled back from the door of death.

2

In that space – the world's fullest dimension
You are
and therefore both I
and my slow fall to the grave
have meaning:
my passage unto death;
the decay turning me to dust of unrepeatable atoms
is a particle of Your Pasch.

3

I wander on the narrow pavement of this earth,
traffic hurtles by,
rockets shoot to space –
in all this
there is a centrifugal flow
(man, a fragment of the world differently set in motion),
this movement does not touch the core of eternity,
it frees no one from death
(man, a fragment of the world differently set in motion),
so I wander on the narrow pavement of this earth,
not turning aside from Your Countenance
unrevealed to me by the world.

4

But death is the experience of the limit,
it has something of annihilation,
I use hope to detach my own self,
I must tear myself away
to stand above annihilation.
And then from all sides they call and will call out:
'You are mad, Paul, you are mad.'*
I wrestle with myself,
with so many others I wrestle
for my hope.
No layer in my memory alone
confirms my hope,
no mirror of passage recreates my hope,
only Your paschal Passage,
welded to the deepest record of my being.

* 'Festus said with a loud voice, "Paul, you are mad; your great learning is
   turning you mad" ' (Acts xxvi, 24).

5

And so I am inscribed in You
by hope,
outside You I cannot exist –
if I place my own self above death
and tear it from the ground of destruction,
it is because the self is inscribed in You
as in the Body which fulfils its power
over each human body
so my own self can be built again;
taken from the ground of my death it has a different countour yet
   so very true,
in which my soul's body and my body's soul are again together,
and my earthbound being rests finally on the Word,
forgetting all pain as does the heart struck by the sudden Wind –
which no man can bear.
And the forests' crowns are rent, and their roots below.
That wind stirred by Your hand now becomes Silence.

6

The atoms of primordial man bind the ancient soil of the world
which I touch with my death
to transplant it, ultimately, into myself,
so that each atom can become your Pasch, or – the *Passage*.

1975

REDEMPTION SEEKING YOUR FORM TO ENTER MAN'S ANXIETY

Veronica

1

The stuff of ordinary days in me
is continually transformed,
seeking an outlet, like a river
weighed to the bottom by its own weight.

Thus the earth flows by, ordinary days remain.
Between me and the earth there is a continuity,
and a hiatus – a most curious crack in the universe,
which perhaps need not grope for fulfilment,
but I, a human creature, must –
like a river seeking its outlet.

The stuff of ordinary days is transformed
in this seeking.
And the outlet – is it thought?

2

(Lighter than earth's elements this element,
in which the others have their likeness
yet unlike them,
stands behind us like a mirror,
staring into mystery,
a hidden link of fulfilment.

Through thought I enter myself into myself,
and continually depart from myself.
I am also at the centre of all
just as thought is at the centre of me.)

3

The world escapes not through thought
into the land of meaning alone.
Animals do not escape, or men, or flowers in vases,
or flowers growing in the meadows
of human loneliness,
or drops of blood on the forehead
of a tortured man –

the land of meaning stretches across
unfathomed love
and leads to it: a step and
an introduction.

4

I wait here for hands with their fill
of daily tasks,
I wait here for hands bearing
ordinary linen.
Raise your hands, Veronica,
to the land of deepest meaning –
raise your hands then,
and touch the face of man.

5

(You did not for a moment wish your act
to be seen as out of the ordinary;
had you so wished, the act
would not have been the same.)

Sister

1

We grow together.
Growing upwards: propped by the heart, green space
moves towards the burdens of wind suddenly cast
onto leaves.
Growing inwards: not growing but learning
how deep your roots thrust,
how much deeper –

We move about in the darkness of roots
thrust into our common soil.
From here I compare the lights above:
the reflex of water on banks of green.

2

No ready footpaths for man.
We are born a thicket
which may burst into flames, into the bush of Moses,
or may wither away.

We are always having to clear the paths,
they will be overgrown again;
they have to be cleared until they are simple
with the mature simplicity of every moment:
for each moment opens the wholeness of time,
as if it stood whole above itself.
You find in it the seed of eternity.

3

When I call you sister
I think that each meeting
contains not only the communion of moments,
but the seed of the same eternity.

Name

1

Your name rose among the people who first noticed your path:
cutting your way you ran.
Did you first learn to cut your way
as the crowds pushed towards the place of Execution –
or did you always know how?
Since when, how long – tell me, Veronica.
The name rose at the moment when your heart
became an image: an image of truth.
Your name rose from your eyes lost in gazing.

2

Sister, you long so much to see,
long so much to feel, your eyes are already there;
you want that image in your heart
to make you wholly feeling.
Vision is love's space.

3

And you say:
close, I want to be so close
that no void can reveal itself apart from You,
so close that your absence cannot return to me
as the denial of myself –
so I run, my heart cuts through the dark
created by the closeness.

4

Nobody stopped you, Veronica.
You are near. This kerchief is now the cry of many hearts,
of all reluctant hearts, no longer cutting their way
because they see your path parallel
to the way of the condemned man.

Redemption

1

Now, they have all gone. You are alone.
On this linen a sign of closeness, where you hide
from your own form,
from the form of life which you cannot accept,
from the crack where a distance is made
for what is innermost.

2

The closeness giving you back your form.
He is gone. When man departs, the closeness flies away
like a bird.
A gap in the heart's flow – and yearning breaks in.

Yearning – hunger for closeness.
The image does not satisfy: it is a sign of distance.
Redemption is the constant closeness of Him Who Has
    Departed.

3

Distance:
it remains with the anxiety of form
which no eye reaches from within,
no face.

Closeness:
you have departed, but through me you walk on.
The distant countenance imprinted on the linen
draws out that peace for which
my restless form searches continually.

Peace: the oneness of existence.

4

The outline of your form, Veronica, stays
traced against the receding day:
it seeks calm in life-giving depth.
This we call redemption.

The darkening linen in your hands draws in the world's anxiety.
Creatures will search for the life-giving source that springs
from your person.
Veronica, sister –
Redemption looked for your form to enter
the anxiety of all men.

STANISLAS

Stanislas (*c.* 1036 – 79) Bishop of Cracow, the patron
saint of Poland. In his conflict with King Boleslas the
Bold he upheld the rights of the Church, as did
Thomas Becket a century later. While celebrating Mass,
Stanislas was murdered by the King.
He was canonized in 1253.
The pilgrimage of Pope John Paul II to his native
country in June 1979 culminated in the celebration of the
900th anniversary of the saint's martyrdom.

I

1

I want to describe the Church, my Church,
born with me, not dying with me –
nor do I die with it,
which always grows beyond me –
the Church: the lowest depth of my existence
and its peak,
the Church – the root which I thrust
into the past and the future alike,
the sacrament of my being in God
who is the Father.

I want to describe the Church,
my Church which bound itself to my land
(this was said: 'Whatever you bind on earth
will be bound in heaven'),
thus to my land my Church is bound.
The land lies in the Vistula basin, the tributaries swell in spring
when the snows thaw in the Carpathians.
The Church bound itself to my land so that all it binds here
should be bound in heaven.

2

There was a man; through him my land saw
it was bound to heaven.
There was such a man, there were such people, such always are –
Through them the earth sees itself in the sacrament
of a new existence. It is a fatherland,
for here the Father's house is begotten and here is born.
I want to describe my Church in the man whose name was
    Stanislas.
And King Boleslas wrote this name with his sword
in the ancient chronicles,
wrote this name with his sword on the cathedral's marble floor
as the streams of blood were flowing
over the marble floor.

3

I want to describe the Church in the name
which baptized the nation again
with the baptism of blood,
that it might later pass through the baptism of other trials,
through the baptism of desires where the hidden is revealed –
the breath of the Spirit;
and in the Name which was grafted
on the soil of human freedom earlier than the name
Stanislas.

4

At that moment, the Body and the Blood being born
on the soil of human freedom were slashed by the king's sword
to the marrow of the priest's word,
slashed at the base of the skull, the living trunk slashed.
The Body and the Blood as yet hardly born,
when the sword struck the metal chalice, and the wheaten bread.

5

The King may have thought: the Church shall not yet be born
  from you,
the nation shall not be born of the word that castigates
the body and the blood;
it will be born of the sword, my sword which severs
your words in mid-flow,
born from the spilled blood – this the King may have thought.

The hidden breath of the Spirit will unify all –
the severed words and the sword, the smashed skull
and the hands dripping with blood – and it says:
go into the future together, nothing shall separate you.
I want to describe my Church in which, for centuries,
the word and the blood go side by side,
united by the hidden breath
of the Spirit.

6

Stanislas may have thought: my word will hurt you
and convert,
you will come as a penitent to the cathedral gate,
emaciated by fasting, enlightened by a voice within,
to join the Lord's table like a prodigal son.
If the word did not convert you, the blood will.
The bishop had perhaps no time to think:
let this cup pass from me.

7

A sword falls on the soil of our freedom.
Blood falls on the soil of our freedom,
And which weighs more?

The first age is at a close,
the second begins.
We take in our hands the outline of the inevitable time.

II

1

In the windows this land rushes by, the trees, the fields run.
The snow glitters on branches, slides off in the sun.
It is green again: young green at first, then ripe, then
green extinguished like candles.
Poland: the land rushes by, in green, in autumn, in snow.
A traveller on foot takes it in – it's a long way
to walk from end to end.
A bird can scarcely cross the land, only a plane
absorbs this space in an hour, squaring the native land
with its wings.

2

The land of hard-won unity, of people seeking their own roads;
this land so long divided between the princes of one clan,
this land subjected to the freedom of each mindful of all.
This land finally torn apart for six generations,
torn on the maps of the world, torn in the fate of her sons.
And through this tearing united in the hearts of the Poles
as no other land.

3

Whence rose this name which he received for his people?
for parents, for the clan, for the bishop's seat in Cracow,
for King Boleslas called the Brave and the Bountiful?
for the twentieth century?

This one name.

Appendix

Among the early poems of Karol Wojtyla which have survived,
there is a manuscript collection entitled 'The Renaissance Psalter:
A Slav Book' (*Renesansowy psałterz: Księga słowiańska*),
completed in 1939 and written when he was still a student of
Polish literature at the University of Cracow. It contains among
others a hymn, 'Magnificat', which is fashioned in an ornate style
of diction and has rhymes and assonances throughout. The
Cracow edition of Wojtyla's poems (*Poezje i dramaty*, 1980)
prints it in the section 'Juvenilia', together with two dramas.

Magnificat
(*Hymn*)

My soul, magnify the glory of the Lord,
Father of great Poetry – and so good.

With wondrous rhythm he fortified my youth,
on an oak anvil he hammered out my song.

Resound, my soul, with the glory of the Lord
who made knowledge of angels, most kindly Maker.

Now at your heavenly banquet, I drain
a chalice with wine overflowing – your servant in prayer:
in gratitude for the angelic glow You lit for my youth
whittling its rough shape from the wood of a linden tree.

You omnipotent, the wondrous woodcarver of saints,
there are many oaks on my road, many birches.
I am a village field, a sunclad flower bed,
a young face jutting from the Tatra rocks.*

I bless your sowing with sunrise and sunset;
Sower, I am your soil – widely scatter your grain –
may a field of rye and a castle of spruce
grow from my youth cradled in yearning and pain.

Let happiness magnify You – a great mystery:
with primordial song you have stretched my lungs,
made my face sink into the blue of the sky,
a shower of music falling on my strings –

and in this melody You came as Christ, a vision.
Look ahead, young Slav, look, the solstice fires!†
The sacred oak is still in leaf, your king has not withered,
but become for the people a lord and a priest.

Magnify the Lord, oh my soul, for your calm foreboding,
for Gothic yearning in spring's incantation,
for youth aflame – wine chalice of elation,
for autumn born in the likeness of heather and stubble.

Magnify Him for poetry, for joy and for pain:
the joy in mastering earth, gold, blue skies,
the passion of generations in words incarnate;
You will harvest this ripeness when it falls and dies.

* A high mountain range in Southern Poland.
† In the original Sobótka, a pagan festival corresponding to St John's Eve, when
  water and fire were celebrated.

The pain is evening sorrow of things half-uttered,
when beauty overwhelms us, and ecstasy is ours,
God bending to the harp – but on a rocky track
a sunbeam breaks, and words lose their power.

Words fail, and I am like a fallen angel,
a statue on marble pedestal – stone on stone –
but You breathed yearning into the marble arms,
the statue longs to take off – angel again.

And I magnify You also for the haven there is in You,
the reward for each song – day of holy quest,
for the joy that sings the hymn of motherhood,
the quiet word of fulfilment – *Eli* manifest!*

Father, be blessed for the angel's sorrow,
for the song that crushes falsehood, for the soul's inspired fight.
Break all love of words in us, and destroy
the puffed-up form parading like a fool.

A Slav troubadour, I walk Your roads and play
to maidens at the solstice, to shepherds with their flock,
but, wide as this vale, my song of prayer
I throw for You only, before your throne of oak.

Blessed are you, oh song among songs,
blessed the soul's sowing and the seeds of light.
Let my soul magnify Him who threw over my shoulders
princely satin, velvet's soft delight.

* *Eli*, as in Christ's cry on the cross: *Eli, Eli, Lama Sabachthani*.

176

Blessed be the Carver-of-saints and prophet and Slav.
Have mercy on me, a publican inspired.
Magnify the Lord, oh my soul, in humble love
singing the hymn: Holy, Holy, Holy!

Now the song is one. Poetry, descend!
The seed like the soul yearns, insatiable.
May my road keep to the shade of oaks and birches,
and may my youthful harvest be pleasing to God.

Slav Book of yearning, on the last day resound
like brass, choirs of the resurrection
in virginal holy song, in poetry that bows
with the hymn of humanity – God's Magnificat.

Cracow, spring–summer, 1939

Sources

With only two exceptions (indicated in the notes), the original texts of the poems translated here from Polish appeared, between 1946 and 1979, mainly in two Catholic periodicals: *Tygodnik Powszechny* (abbreviated as *TP*) and *Znak*, both published in Cracow. These sources have been collated with the edition of *Poezje i dramaty*, Cracow, 1980.

For clarity's sake the pen names used by Karol Wojtyla are indicated in headings.

★ ★ ★

Over this your white grave (Nad Twoją białą mogiłą), the opening poem from the manuscript collection, 'The Renaissance Psalter: A Slav Book' (*Renesansowy psałterz: Księga słowiańska*), 1939, first published in *Poezje i dramaty*.

SONG OF THE HIDDEN GOD (*Pieśń o Bogu ukrytym*), completed in 1944. Parts of this cycle were printed in *Głos Karmelu*, 1946, nos. 1–2; 1947, nos. 3 and 5, without signature. The full text is printed in *Poezje i dramaty*.

Shores of silence (*Wybrzeża pełne ciszy*)
Song of the inexhaustible sun (*Pieśń o słońcu niewyczerpanym*)

Under the pen name Andrzej Jawień

SONG OF THE BRIGHTNESS OF WATER (*Pieśń o blasku wody*, published in *TP*, 7 May 1950):
Looking into the well at Sichar (*Nad studnią w Sychem*)
When you open your eyes deep in a wave (*Gdy otworzysz oczy w głębi fali*)
Words spoken by the woman at the well, on departing (*Słowa niewiasty u studni, które wypowiedziała odchodząc*)
Later recollection of the meeting (*Późniejsze rozpamiętywanie spotkania*)

Conversations he had within her: and the people from the wall of evening (*Rozmowy, które prowadził w niej on i ludzie ze ściany wieczoru*)
The Samaritan woman (*Samarytanka*)
The Samaritan woman meditates (*Rozważania ponowne*)
Song of the brightness of water (*Pieśń o blasku wody*)

MOTHER (*Matka*, published in *TP*, 10 December 1950):
First moment of the glorified body (*Pierwsza chwila uwielbionego ciała*)
Words which grow into me (*Słowa, które rozrastają się we mnie*)
Her amazement at her only child (*Zdumienie nad Jednorodzonym*)
Mature attention (*Skupienie dojrzałe*)
John beseeches her (*Prośba Jana*)
Space which remains in you (*Przestrzeń, która w Tobie została*)
The song opens (*Otwarcie pieśni*)
Embraced by new time (*Objęta nowym czasem*)

THOUGHT–STRANGE SPACE (*Myśl jest przestrzenią dziwną*, published in *TP*, 19 October 1952):
Thought's resistance to words (*Opór stawiany wyrazom przez myśli*)
Sentences snatched from a conversation long ago, now recollected (*Dawna rozmowa, z której teraz niektóre zdania zapamiętane wyrywam*)
Words' resistance to thought (*Opór stawiany myślom przez wyrazy*)
Jacob (*Jakub*)
Space necessary for the drops of spring rain (*Przestrzeń potrzebna kroplom wiosennego deszczu*)
Error (*Błąd*)
Proper weight (*Ciężar właściwy*)
For the companions of the road (*Dla towarzyszów drogi*)

THE QUARRY (*Kamieniołom*, published in *Znak*, November 1957), written in 1956:
Material (*Tworzywo*)
Inspiration (*Natchnienie*)
Participation (*Uczestnictwo*)
(In memory of a fellow-worker) (*Pamięci towarzysza pracy*)

PROFILES OF A CYRENEAN (*Profile Cyrenejczyka*, published in *TP*, 23 March 1958), written in 1957:
> I: Before I could discern many profiles (*Zanim jeszcze potrafiłem rozróżnić wiele profilów*)
> II: Now I begin to discern individual profiles (*Teraz już zaczynam rozróżniać poszczególne profile*)
> Melancholic (*Melancholik*)
> Schizoid (*Schizotymik*)
> The blind (*Niewidomi*)
> Actor (*Aktor*)
> Girl disappointed in love (*Dziewczyna zawiedziona w miłości*)
> Children (*Dzieci*)
> Man's thoughts (*Myśli człowieka*)
> Description of man (*Rysopis człowieka*)
> The car factory worker (*Robotnik z fabryki samochodów*)
> The armaments factory worker (*Robotnik z fabryki broni*)
> Magdalene (*Magdalena*)
> Man of emotion (*Człowiek emocji*)
> Man of intellect (*Człowiek intelektu*)
> Man of will (*Człowiek woli*)
> III: Simon of Cyrene (*Szymon z Cyreny*)

THE BIRTH OF CONFESSORS (*Narodziny wyznawców*, published in *Znak*, November 1963, together with 'The Church' [see below] and signed 'A.J.'). Written in 1961:
> A bishop's thoughts on giving the sacrament of confirmation in a mountain village (*Myśli biskupa udzielającego sakramentu bierzmowania w pewnej podgórskiej wsi*)
> Thoughts of a man receiving the sacrament of confirmation in a mountain village (*Myśli człowieka przyjmującego sakrament bierzmowania w pewnej podgórskiej wsi*)

THE CHURCH (*Kościół* [*Fragmenty*], published in *Znak*, November 1963, and signed 'A.J.'), also has a subtitle, 'Shepherds and Springs' (*Pasterze i źródła*):
> Wall (*Sciana*)
> Abyss (*Przepaść*)
> The Negro (*Murzyn*)
> Marble floor (*Posadzka*)
> The crypt (*Krypta*)
> Synodus (*Synodus*)
> Gospel (*Ewangelia*)

Springs and hands (*Źródła i ręce*)
Two cities (*Dwa miasta*)

JOURNEY TO THE HOLY PLACES (*Wędrówka do miejsc świętych*,
published in *Znak*, June 1965, and signed 'A.J.'). The author
visited the Holy Land in December 1963.
Mount of Olives (*Oliveti*)
The desert of Judea (*Pustynia judzka*)
Identities (*Tożsamości*)
One tree (*Jedno drzewo*)
The place within (*Miejsce wewnętrzne*)

EASTER VIGIL, 1966 (*Wigilia wielkanocna 1966*, published in
Znak, April 1966, and signed 'A.J.'):
I: Invocation (*Inwokacja*)
A conversation with oneself begins (*Rozpoczyna się rozmowa z
sobą*)
A conversation with God begins (*Rozpoczyna się rozmowa z
Bogiem*)
A conversation with man begins: the meaning of things
(*Rozpoczyna się rozmowa z człowiekiem, spór o znaczenie
rzeczy*)
Invocation to Man who became the body of history (*Właściwa
inwokacja czyli wołanie do człowieka, który stał się ciałem
historii*)
II: A tale of a wounded tree (*Opowieść o drzewie zranionym*)
III: Seams (*Spojenia*)
IV: Development of language (*Rozwój języka*)
V: Echo of the firstborn cry (*Echo pierworodnego płaczu*)
VI: Ritual (*Obrzęd*)
VII: Easter Vigil, 1966 (*Wigilia wielkanocna 1966*)

Under the pen name Stanisław Andrzej Gruda

THINKING MY COUNTRY (*Myśląc ojczyzna*, published in *Znak*,
January–February 1979), written in 1974:
All round they speak with tongues (*Gdy dokoła mówią
językami*)
I still hear (*Słyszę jeszcze dźwięk kosy*)
I reach the heart of the drama (*Docieram do serca dramatu*)
Refrain (*Refren*)
Thinking my Country I return to the tree (*Myśląc ojczyzna,
powracam w stronę drzewa*)

MEDITATION ON DEATH (*Rozważanie o śmierci*, published in *Znak*, March 1975):
Thoughts on maturing (*Myśli o dojrzewaniu*)
Mysterium paschale (*Mysterium paschale*)
Fear which is at the beginning (*Bojaźń, która leży u początku*)
Hope reaching beyond the limit (*Nadzieja, która sięga poza kres*)

REDEMPTION SEEKING YOUR FORM TO ENTER MAN'S
ANXIETY (*Odkupienie szuka twego kształtu, by wejść w niepokój wszystkich ludzi*, published in *Znak*, October 1979):
Veronica (*Weronika*)
Sister (*Siostra*)
Name (*Imię*)
Redemption (*Odkupienie*)

STANISLAS (*Stanisław*, published in *Znak*, July–August 1979).

Appendix

Magnificat, a hymn from the manuscript collection, 'The Renaissance Psalter' (*Renesansowy psałterz: Księga słowiańska*, 1939), first published in *Poezje i dramaty*.

ACKNOWLEDGEMENTS

Authorization to translate these poems from the Polish original was graciously granted by the author.

I wish to express my gratitude to the following people who have helped in various ways: Bogumil W. Andrzejewski, Rosamond Batchelor, Ann Irving, the late Leszek Kukulski, Father J. Mirewicz, SJ, and Anthony Whittome of Hutchinson.

My very special thanks go to Carol O'Brien for her encouragement and advice during my work on the poems.

J.P.

ABOUT THE AUTHOR

KAROL WOJTYLA was born in 1920 in Wadowice, Poland, a small town near Cracow. In 1938 he began to study literature at Cracow's Jagellonian University, simultaneously pursuing an interest in drama. The outbreak of World War II interrupted his literary studies, but he continued to act, joining a group called the Rhapsodic Theater. In 1941, following his father's death, he worked for a time in the stone quarries and, later, in a chemical plant. It was also during the war that he began to study for the priesthood, enrolling in 1942 in Jagellonian University's underground Theological Department. Hidden from the Gestapo for the remainder of the German occupation by the then Archbishop of Cracow, Wojtyla was ordained a priest on November 1, 1946. After taking a philosophy degree at Rome's Angelicum, he taught theology and ethics at the Catholic University of Lublin. In 1958 he was named bishop of Cracow, became archbishop in 1964, and in 1967 was appointed cardinal. On October 16, 1978, Karol Wojtyla was elected Pope, taking the name John Paul II. In addition to the poems in this volume, he has written six plays, numerous essays, and is the author of several works of philosophy, including *Love and Responsibility, Sign and Contradiction* and *The Acting Person.*

ABOUT THE TRANSLATOR

JERZY PETERKIEWICZ was born in Fabianki, Poland. A poet, novelist, critic and biographer, he was educated in Warsaw and at St. Andrews and King's College, London, and was until 1980 Professor of Polish Literature at the University of London. He was chosen as translator of Karol Wojtyla's poetry by a special Papal Commission.